The Travel Tourism Teaching Dictionary

Verité Reily Collins

Edited by David Leith
Ben Long

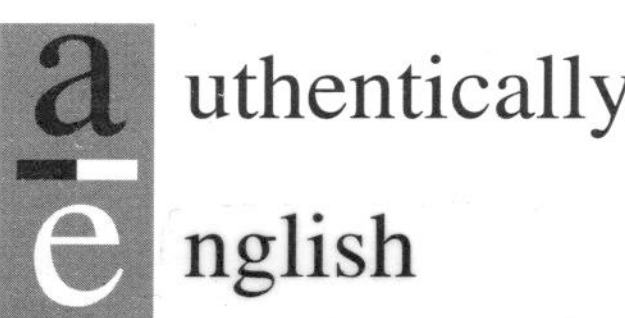

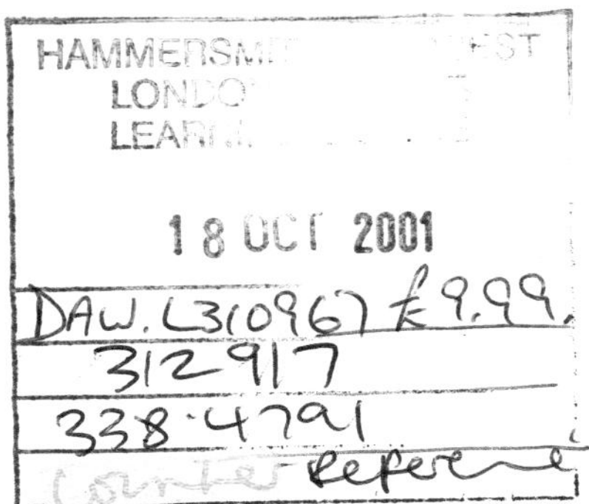

Consultant Editor - David Leith
Production Editor - Ben Long
Additional Contributions - Pam Todd

Published by:
Authentically English
60 Albert Court
Prince Consort Road
London, SW7 2BH.

ISBN 0-952-75095-3

We would like to thank many people who have helped with the publishing of this text: in particular Alan Bowen and the ABTA staff at Newman Street, The Association of Independent Tour Operators, Valda Hurley of The British Airline Pilots' Association, the staff of Kensington and Chelsea library, The Anglesea Arms, David Porter MSc.,Micky Adams, John Cottier and Brian Cooper.

International Phonetic Alphabet

At the beginning of each letter in the dictionary you will find the capital letter (upper case), the small letter (lower case) and the name of each letter in relation to the Phonetic/ International Alphabet.

Throughout the world, all people that communicate by radio use the phonetic alphabet for transmitting information in order to aid clarity and accuracy. Flight numbers for airlines are an example for the need for clarity and accuracy. The flight number VS001 from London to New York (Virgin Atlantic 001) would be pronounced by air traffic control and the pilot 'Victor Sierra Zero Zero Wun'. This prevents any misinterpretation of the flight number that may cause danger or any unnecessary confusion with other aircraft and their respective flight numbers. The letter 'V' could be misinterpreted with 'D','B','C' etc., and also the letter 'S' could be misinterpreted with 'F', thus, the use of the phonetic alphabet. The numbers are pronounced in this way for exactly the same reason, and a list of the numbers is written at the end of this short piece.

Another very useful factor that the phonetic alphabet has, is that it acts as a form of international communication due to it's worldwide usage. Different nationalities who speak different languages can understand one another through this alphabet, as it is a global method for communication.

A	Alpha	U	Uniform
B	Bravo	V	Victor
C	Charlie	W	Whisky
D	Delta	X	X-Ray
E	Echo	Y	Yankee
F	Foxtrot	Z	Zulu
G	Golf		
H	Hotel		
I	India	0	Zero
J	Juliet	1	Wun
K	Kilo	2	Too
L	Lima	3	Tree
M	Mike	4	Fower
N	November	5	Fife
O	Oscar	6	Six
P	Papa	7	Seven
Q	Quebec	8	Ait
R	Romeo	9	Niner
S	Sierra	Hundred	Hun Dred
T	Tango	Thousand	Tousand

Dictionary for the Tourism Industry

The following section is the central part of the publication. Within this section, there are approximately 1800 words, phrases, acronyms and abbreviations with their definitions, that are directly relevant to, and associated with the travel and tourism industry. You will find some words have more than one meaning in relation to the industry, and this will be clearly defined in a numerical form. Each word will have either v, n, adj., adv. after it, that will describe to the user whether the word is utilised contextually within the travel and tourism industry as a verb, noun, adjective or adverb respectively. There will be many abbreviations and acronyms and these will be defined by acr. - acronym and abbr. - abbreviation. The names of charities, and other organisations will be defined by org. - organisation. Slang terms will also be marked as such.

Abbreviations used in this dictionary.

abbr.	abbreviation
acr.	acronym
adj.	adjective
adv.	adverb
e.g.	for example
etc.	et cetera
Fr.	French
Ger.	German
i.e.	for instance
km	kilometre
k.p.h.	kilometres per hour
m.p.h.	miles per hour
n	noun
n.b.	nota bene: note well
org.	organisation
slang	slang
UK	United Kingdom
US/A	United States of America
v	verb

Aa - Alpha

AA (abbr.) Automobile Association. Vehicle breakdown recovery service (UK).

A.A.A. (abbr.) American Automobile Association (US).

A.A.C. (abbr.) Association of Airline Consolidators.

A.A.I.B. (abbr.) Air Accident Investigation Branch.

A.B.A. (abbr.) Aircharter Brokers Association.

Abacus (n) C.R.S. for airlines including Singapore International Airlines, Thai Airways and Cathay Pacific.

A.B.C. (abbr.) Advanced Booking Charter.

able-bodied passengers (n) Passengers permitted/requested to sit by emergency escape exits, who are capable of assisting with the evacuation of aircraft or ship.

Abonnement (n) European rail pass allowing the holder unlimited travel within a certain period of time (Fr.).

abort (v) Emergency procedure. To stop an aircraft takeoff when it has already started, because to continue would be dangerous.

above-the-line (n) Advertising industry terminology. Advertising using traditional media including television, radio, magazines, newspapers and posters.

A.B.P. (abbr.) **1.** Associated British Ports. **2.** Able-Bodied Passengers.

A.B.P.C.O. (abbr.) Association of British Professional Conference Organisers.

abroad (adv.) In a country or countries other than one's own.

ABTA (acr.) Association of British Travel Agents.

ABTAC (acr.) Association of British Travel Agents Certificate.

Abtech (n) Service provided by ABTA for it's members offering advice on the use of I.T. (Information Technology) in travel agents and tour operators.

A.B.T.O.F. (abbr.) Association of British Tour Operators in France.

A.B.T.O.T. (abbr.) Association of Bonded Travel Organisers Trust.

access (n) The right to visit a property or premises.

accessibility (n) **1.** Ease of use of travel from one particular location to another. This can be measured by distance travelled, cost of travel, the time taken to travel, ease of transferring from one form of transport to another. **2.** The level of ease or difficulty of access for disabled people.

accident insurance (n) Insurance carried by travellers to pay for emergency medical attention when away from their home country.

accommodation (n) Rooms that are provided for living and sleeping.

accompanying person (n) A person who accompanies a delegate to a conference, meeting or exhibition who does not attend any of the formal events with the delegate.

accreditation (n) **1.** Official appointment or authorisation to act as an agent. **2.** Authorisation for journalist to cover an event.

acculturation (n) The effect of different cultures on each other when they come into contact, either by direct meeting of peoples or through the influence of the media, and the changes which result.

ACE (acr.) Association for Conferences and Events.

acknowledge (v) To let someone know you have received and understood their message.

ACORN (acr.) Method that looks at people's lifestyles - A Classification Of Residential Neighbourhoods.

acoustics (n) Relating to the quality of hearing or sound reproduction.

ACT (acr.) Association of Couriers in

ACT (acr.) Association of Couriers in Tourism.
A.C.T.E. (abbr.) Association of Corporate Travel Executives.
act of God (n) Event caused by natural forces and beyond human control such as earthquakes, floods etc..
active (adj.) Term used when interpreting. The active language is the language into which all interpreters will translate.
activity holiday (n) Holiday where guests take part in a sporting or other energetic activities.
A.C.T.O. (abbr.) Association of Camping Tour Operators.
A.D. (abbr.) **1.** Anno Domini. Signifies after the death of Christ, used in dates - i.e 2000 AD. **2.** Air worthiness Directive. This is given when an aircraft has some defect that officials consider hazardous. The aircraft is not permitted to fly until the defect is corrected.
AD75 (abbr.) 75 per cent Agent's Discount. IATA allows each appointed IATA agency to be issued with two 75 per cent discounted tickets per calendar year by each IATA airline.
ad hoc (adj.) Made by special arrangement.
ad hoc interpreting (n) When an interpreter translates conversation in a small group.
adaptor (n) Device that enables users of electrical goods to connect to foreign power supply outlets.
add-on (n) Additional or extra.
adjoining (n) Rooms that are next to each other.
admin. (abbr.) Abbreviation for administration.
administration (n) The office duties of a company or organisation - e.g. photocopying, faxing.
admission charge (n) Fee payable in order to enter a venue.
adobe (n) Bricks of sun-dried earth or clay, used as building materials.
advance booking/reservation (n) Booking prior to the start of a holiday.
adventure holiday (n) Holiday with a major sporting/activity content.
Advertising Standards Authority (org.) Regulating body that monitors the standard of advertisements to make sure that they are truthful and not offensive.
A.E.O. (abbr.) Association of Exhibition Organisers.
aerodrome (n) Place where aircraft land and takeoff. Smaller than an airport and mainly used by private aircraft.
A.F.A. (abbr.) Association of Flight Attendants (US).
A.F.C.A.C. (abbr.) African Civil Aviation Commission.
affinity group (n) Special interest group.
affirmative (adj.) Yes.
AFORR (acr.) Association of Foreign Railway Representatives.
aft (adv.) In, near, to, towards the stern or rear of a ship.
agency agreement (n) Formal arrangement between travel agency and principal supplier detailing commission and other terms of supply - i.e. An agreement between a travel agent and a tour operator or service company.
agenda (n) List of topics/subjects to be discussed at a meeting.
A.G.L. (abbr.) Above Ground Level.
agro-town (n) A town of population up to 20,000 people, with agriculture as the main economic activity.
AIDA (acr.) Process by which consumers go through when purchasing a product - Awareness, Interest, Desire, Action.
A.I.I.C. (abbr.) Association Internationale des Interprétes de Conférence (Fr.). International Association of Conference

aileron (n) Hinged flap at trailing edge of wings of an aircraft which moves up and down to induce banking or turning.

A.I.P.C. (abbr.) Association Internationale des Palais des Congres.

aircraft leasing (n) When an aircraft is rented to an airline or organisation. See also dry lease and wet lease.

air frame (n) The structure of an aircraft excluding the engines and accessories.

Air Freedom Rights (n) Rights established for airlines by 1944 Chicago Convention. First freedom - to overfly one country en-route to another. Second freedom - to make a technical stop in another country. Third freedom - to carry passengers from the native country to another country. Fourth freedom - to carry passengers to the native country from another country. Fifth freedom - to carry passengers between two countries by an airline of a third on a route with origin/destination in its native country. Sixth freedom - to carry passengers between two countries by an airline of a third on two routes connecting in its native country. Seventh freedom - to carry passengers between two countries by an airline of a third on a route outside its home country. Eighth freedom - (Cabotage) to carry passengers within a country by an airline of another country on a route with origin/destination in its native country.

air hostess (n) Female who serves and looks after passengers on an aircraft.

air miles (n) **1.** Loyalty points earned by passengers when travelling on certain airlines, and also in exchange for buying some goods. Air miles, when redeemed give holders tickets valid for air travel. **2.** Trading name of the company that administers this points scheme for British Airways (UK).

air miss (n) When two aircraft unintentionally fly dangerously close to each other.

air pocket (n) Partial vacuum in the air which can cause an aircraft to lose height suddenly and without warning.

air terminal (n) Airport building that provides services to passengers arriving and departing on airline flights.

air traffic (n) All aircraft in flight or operating on the manoeuvring area of a runway.

air traffic control (n) The official authority in charge of aircraft movements into and out of airports, and controlling aircraft movement in the airspace in their allocated zone or sector.

air traffic controller (n) Person working in air traffic control monitoring aircraft movements and giving instruction by radio to pilots to ensure that aircraft do not collide in the air or on the ground.

air waybill (n) List of goods or people being transported by air.

air-conditioned (adj.) Area cooled by means of refrigerated air.

air-cooled (adj.) Area cooled by a current of forced air.

airbridge (n) Corridor brought to the doors of aircraft to allow people to exit and to enter.

aircraft (n) Normally refers to an airplane (US) or aeroplane (UK), however, it can be used to describe any form of airborne transport.

aircrew (n) Pilot and other people on an aircraft who are needed to fly the aircraft and look after any passengers on-board.

airfare (n) Cost of a journey in an aircraft.

airfield (n) Small aerodrome, often privately owned, generally with no official presence - i.e. no customs, etc..

airlane (n) Officially recognised route through the air used by aircraft.

airline (n) Company that provides regular flights for passengers or freight.

airline codes (n) Reference letters used

to represent airlines on timetables and on tickets etc. - e.g. BA = British Airways, AF = Air France. See also airline codings section.

airliner (n) Large aircraft designed to carry paying passengers.

airpass (n) Special airfares for visitors from outside a country.

airplane (n) Aeroplane. Aircraft that has at least one engine and wings (US).

airport (n) Place where aircraft land and takeoff, that has facilities for passengers and often customs and immigration.

airport hotel (n) Hotel built on perimeter of airport, for use by air travellers.

airship (n) Large elongated balloon, containing a gas that is lighter than air which enables it to fly. Airships usually have a cabin to carry passengers beneath the balloon and an engine to power them.

airsick (adj.) Motion sickness caused by flying.

airside (n) Area of an airport after check-in, that is between customs and aircraft - e.g. duty free shops are airside.

airspace (n) The air or sky above a country regarded as belonging to that country. Aircraft have to obtain permission to enter a country's airspace, as they would if they docked at a port or entered by road.

airspeed (n) Measurement in knots of the speed of an aircraft through the air.

airstream (n) A current of air or a wind.

airstrip (n) A strip of land which is used by aircraft, often small private aircraft, for takeoff and landing.

airway (n) Part or all of a controlled area in the form of a 'corridor' through the air. An airway has radio navigation aids throughout its route to help guide aircraft along it.

airworthiness certificates (n) Written permission given under government regulations to show that an aircraft is working to the required standard.

aisle (n) Passage between seating - e.g. in an aircraft, train, theatre, church or at an exhibition.

A.I.T.O. (abbr.) Association of Independent Tour Operators.

à la carte (adj.) Menu providing a choice of separate items.

alarm call (n) Telephone or verbal message booked in advance, normally used to wake up a person.

alien (adj.) **1.** A person who is not a legal citizen of the country in which they live. **2.** A person who belongs to a different country. **3.** Person or being from another planet.

alight (v) Get down from/leave vehicle/transport.

alliance (n) When airlines form an alliance to share routes. See Code Share.

allocate (v) Officially give out or assign seats, places or rooms.

allocation (n) Section, rooms, seats etc. reserved for a particular group or operator.

A.L.P.A. (abbr.) Air Line Pilots' Association (US).

alpine (adj.) In, or of mountains.

alps (n) Large mountains.

alternative airport (n) Any airport to which a flight may be diverted if a landing at the original destination is no longer possible.

alternative tourism (n) Tourism designed not to damage the environment, that is 'ecologically friendly'.

altitude (n) The measurement in feet of the distance above sea level that an aircraft is flying.

A.L.V.A. (abbr.) Association of Leading Visitor Attractions.

A.M. (abbr.) Notation for the time between midnight and midday (morning).

Amadeus (n) C.R.S. for airlines including Lufthansa, Iberia, Air France, Air Inter & SAS.

ambassador (n) Person sent to a foreign

country to be the senior representative of their own country.

ambulance (n) Vehicle used for carrying sick or injured people to medical centre or hospital.

amenity (n) Something that is provided for people's enjoyment - e.g. restaurant, leisure centre.

amenity kit (n) Complementary bag given out to airline passengers (usually Business or First Class) containing useful or luxury products designed to entice travellers to use the airline again. Often known as 'goodies bags'.

amidships (adv.) Middle part of a ship.

amphitheatre (n) Open-air theatre with rising rows of seats - often Greek or Roman.

amplification (n) Relating to increase in strength or intensity of sound.

A.M.T.A. (abbr.) Association of Multiple Travel Agents.

Amtrak (org.) Railways organisation in the United States of America.

amusement park (n) Theme park or venue where visitors pay admission fee. It may offer different forms of entertainment, including rides and other activities.

analyse (v) The examination of an organisation's marketing process in order to assess the selling of it's products and services.

anchor **1.** (n) A heavy metal hooked object attached to a boat/ship/yacht that is dropped over the side to prevent it from moving. **2.** (v) To prevent something from moving, keeping it in a fixed place (usually associated with a boat).

animation slides (n) Projection technique which creates an illusion of movement when slides (photographic transparencies) are used in rapid succession.

animator (n) Person who entertains holiday-makers (Fr.).

announcement (n) Official statement.

Antarctic (n) Cold regions surrounding the South Pole.

Antarctic Circle (n) Line of latitude 66.5° South. South of which are the Antarctic regions.

anticyclone (n) An area of high barometric pressure, commonly several thousands of kilometres in diameter, with the winds blowing outwards, giving settled weather with few clouds.

ANTOR (acr.) Association of National Tourist Office Representatives.

A.O.A. (abbr.) Airport Operators Association.

A.O.C. (abbr.) Airline Operators' Committee.

A.O.N.B. (abbr.) Area of Outstanding Natural Beauty.

A/P (abbr.) Airport.

AP (abbr.) Via Atlantic and Pacific.

A.P. (abbr.) American Plan = full board accommodation, which includes meals.

A.P.C.O. (abbr.) Association of Pleasure Craft Operators.

aperitif (n) An alcoholic drink that is served before a formal meal.

APEX (acr.) Advance Purchase Excursion Fare. Ticket for air, rail or ferry travel with limitations.

A.P.N. (abbr.) Advance Passenger Notice.

Apollo (n) C.R.S. for airlines including United Airlines.

appeal (n) Positive factors that attract customers to a facility or attraction.

appointment (n) Final part of a recruitment process, a successful candidate for a job will be 'appointed' the position.

approach (n) Final part of a flight when aircraft is about to land at an airport.

approved (adj.) Agreed or endorsed.

approx. (abbr.) Approximately.

approximately (adj.) Near to correct or accurate.

A.P.R.O. (abbr.) Airline Public Relations Organisation.

apron (n) Area in front of terminal where aircraft park to load passengers.

A.P.S.C. (abbr.) Atlantic Passenger Steamship Conference.

A.P.T.G. (abbr.) Association of Professional Tourist Guides.

aquaplaning (adj.) When an aircraft skids on a wet runway at speed causing the wheels of the aircraft to lift slightly in the water, causing loss of grip.

aquifer (n) Rock which will hold water and let it pass through.

archipelago (n) Group of islands and the surrounding sea.

Arctic (n) Cold regions surrounding the North Pole.

Arctic Circle (n) Line of latitude 66.5° North. North of which are the Arctic regions.

area of outstanding natural beauty (n) An area, supervised by the relevant local authority, in which development is very carefully considered, so that the quality of the landscape is not diminished.

ARELS (acr.) Association of Recognised English Language Schools (UK).

armrests (n) Support for arms at the edge (sides) of a seat.

A.R.R. (abbr.) Average Room Rate.

arrivals 1. (n) Area passengers enter after disembarkation from transport and Customs clearance etc.. **2.** (adj.) People expected to, or having recently arrived.

ARTAC (acr.) Alliance of Independent Travel Agents.

A.S.A. (abbr.) **1.** Air Services Agreement. An agreement between two or more states regulating air services between them. **2.** Advertising Standards Authority.

A.S.A.E. (abbr.) American Society of Association Executives.

A.S.G. (abbr.) Air Safety Group.

A.S.M. (abbr.) Available Seat Miles.

asset (n) All property belonging to a company or business.

assicuratione (n) Permit for Couriers to work in Italy (Italian).

assign (v) Allocate particular seat or workload etc..

A.S.T.A. (abbr.) American Society of Travel Agents.

AT (abbr.) Via ATlantic.

at one time capacity (n) The maximum amount of people that a tourist attraction can accommodate at any one time.

A.T.A. (abbr.) Air Transport Association.

A.T.C. (abbr.) **1.** Air Traffic Control. **2.** Australian Tourist Commission.

A.T.D. (abbr.) Actual Time of Departure.

Athens Convention (n) International Agreement setting liability of shipping companies in respect of loss or damage to luggage and injury or death of passengers.

A.T.L. (abbr.) Air Transport Licence.

ATOL (acr.) Air Travel Organisers Licence.

atoll (n) A ring shaped island or a group of islands made of coral that has a lagoon in the middle.

A.T.R.F. (abbr.) Air Travel Reserve Fund. Organisers of group air travel must have an Air Travel Organiser's Licence, which involves a substantial bond enabling the public to be protected against financial failure of the operator. If this bond should prove insufficient, the public is further protected against loss of their money by the ATRF.

A.T.S. (abbr.) Air Traffic Services. Organisation which has responsibility for flight information, alerting service, air traffic advisory service, air traffic control, approach control, etc..

A.T.T. (abbr.) Association of Tourism Teachers.

A.T.T.A. (abbr.) Africa Travel & Tourism Association.

A.T.T.F. (abbr.) Air Travel Trust Fund. Money made available by the Civil Aviation Authority (C.A.A.) to companies which have an Air Travel Organisers Licence (ATOL) when a bond lodged by the company is not enough to meet the value of claims made against it.

attraction (n) Venue, place or tour destination that is of interest to visitors.

A.U.C. (abbr.) Air transport Users Committee.

audio conferencing (n) Discussion between three or more people in separate areas, who communicate using a telephone so each person can communicate. The practical maximum for this system is six people.

audio-visual aids (n) See A.V..

auditorium (n) The area where the audience sits in a theatre, hall, etc..

aurora borealis (n) Bands of coloured and white flashing lights seen in the sky north of the Arctic Circle.

authorise (v) To give permission to a person.

authorised (n) Officially appointed representative or officially approved action.

autobahn (n) German motor/highway.

autocue (n) Reflecting sheet of glass in front of a speaker or lecturer, showing script which can be read to give audiences the impression that they are not using notes.

auto-pilot (n) Mechanical means of piloting an aircraft. Only used when aircraft is cruising and no major adjustments have to be made. Often known as 'George'.

autoroute (n) French motorway /highway.

autostrada (n) Italian motorway /highway.

A.V. (abbr.) Audio-visual aids are designed to accompany a speaker at a conference or meeting to help convey a message or lecture etc.. Audio-visual aids include - film, video, slides, OHP, charts etc..

avalanche (n) A rapidly descending mass of snow, ice or rock, moving down a mountain or the sides of a valley.

aviation fuel (n) Fuel used in aircraft. Usually very high octane petrol for piston engined aircraft, or kerosene (paraffin) for jet turbine engines.

A.X.O. (abbr.) Agents eXchange Order.

Bb - Bravo

B.A.A. (abbr.) British Airports Authority. Company that owns and operates some of world's busiest airports such as Heathrow and Gatwick.

BABA (acr.) Book A Bed Ahead (service offered in T.I.C.s).

baby-sitter (n) Person who looks after a child on behalf of the parents for a short time.

B.A.C.A. (abbr.) Baltic Air Charter Association.

B.A.C.D. (abbr.) British Association of Conferences Destinations.

back of house (n) Working area of hotel not used by guests - e.g. store rooms, kitchens, laundry.

back projection (n) System where an image is projected onto the back of a screen instead of from the front.

back to back (adj.) When tour or charter leaves one group at destination while collecting the previous group.

B.A.C.T. (abbr.) British Association of Conference Towns.

badge (n) Identifying label or tag worn on clothes on which the wearer's identity is displayed.

baggage (n) Luggage, personal possessions packed in bags or cases for travelling.

baggage allowance (n) The amount (weight) of luggage than can be taken by a passenger on a commercial without incurring additional cost. See free luggage.

baggage check (n) Receipt issued by a carrier for the luggage of a passenger.
baggage room (n) See Luggage Room.
baggage tag (n) Luggage label. Label attached to baggage etc. so that it can be identified.
B.A.H.A. (abbr.) British Activity Holiday Association.
BAHREP (acr.) British Association of Hotel Representatives.
bail bond (n) Insurance document that covers payment for bail if a coach is involved in an accident (Spanish).
balance of payment (n) Amount still due on a bill or invoice.
balance of payments (n) The difference in a nation's economy between the income from the exports and the cost of imports.
balance sheet (n) A financial summary of what a business or company owes and what it is owns.
balcony (n) **1.** A structure attached to the side of a building with a wall or railing around, it is situated above the ground floor to enable people to sit or stand in the open air. **2.** The area of seating in a theatre or a cinema that is above the main seating area.
BALPA (acr.) British Airline Pilots' Association.
B.A.L.P.P.A. (abbr.) British Association of Leisure Parks Piers and Attractions.
B and B (abbr.) Bed and Breakfast.
bandstand (n) Round stage, raised above the ground, with a roof, used by bands when giving concerts outdoors.
bank draft (n) Cheque (check US) drawn on a bank by a person. The amount of the bank draft must be paid in advance and therefore must be honoured by the issuing bank.
bank holiday (n) Statutory holiday during which banks are closed.
banner (n) Long strip of cloth or material with a message or slogan written or drawn on it.
banquet (n) Large formal seated meal normally for a special occasion.
banqueting manager (n) Person in charge of organising banquets, in an hotel or conference venue. They are responsible for the staff, supply of food and drink, maintenance, and finance of their department.
bar code (n) Computer read identification strip. It is now used to help identify luggage.
barbecue (n) Outdoor meal where food is cooked on an open charcoal fire.
bareboat charter (n) Yacht for hire without crew.
barge (n) Similar to a narrow boat that is commonly seen in Europe. It is wider than a narrow boat due to the fact that the canals are wider in Europe than in UK. - See narrow boat.
barman (n) Person who works behind a bar serving drinks to customers.
barometer (n) Instrument for measuring atmospheric pressure used for predicting the weather.
barrage (n) A structure built across a river or estuary in order to slow or stop the flow of water.
barrier reef (n) A coral reef stretching along a line parallel with the coastline but separated from it by a wide, deep lagoon.
bartender (n) Barman (US).
B.A.R.U.K. (abbr.) Board of Airline Representatives in the UK.
BASI (acr.) British Association of Ski Instructors.
bassinet (n) Baby's bed or cot (US).
bastion (n) A defensive fortification which is part of a castle.
B.A.W.T.A. (abbr.) British Association of Wholesale Tour Agents.
bay (n) Part of the coast which curves inwards.
B-B-Q (abbr.) Barbecue.

the edge of the sea or a lake.

beacon (n) Marker or transmitter used for navigation. A system of navigational beacons transmitting on VHF, radiates a series of bearings. These are picked up on the aircraft's radio compass. Every time the aircraft crosses a beacon, the co-pilot reports the time it was crossed, height and estimated time for crossing the next beacon. The air traffic controller will not let the next aircraft cross that beacon until the previous aircraft is clear.

B.E.C.A. (abbr.) British Exhibition Contractors Association.

bed and breakfast (n) Accommodation providing bed and a morning meal, often in a private house (UK).

bed night (n) One person spending one night in accommodation.

bell boy/hop (n) Porter (US).

bell captain (n) Hall porter (US).

below-the-line (n) Advertising industry terminology. Advertising by direct promotion such as leaflet distribution, exhibitions, sponsorship and merchandising.

benefits (n) The positive factors that customers receive from using an organisation's products and services - e.g. comfort and value for money.

Benelux (n) Term for Belgium, Netherlands and Luxembourg, which is derived from their names.

bequest (n) The value of money and property that is left to another person or organisation in a will.

Bermuda Agreement (n) Air service agreement between Britain and USA in 1946, relating to services between the two countries, and often used as basis for other bilateral agreements.

Bermuda Triangle (n) A section of the Atlantic ocean between Florida, Puerto Rico and Bermuda, where aircraft and ships are said to have disappeared.

berth (n) **1.** Place where a ship ties up or anchors. **2.** Sleeping place on transport (ship, train etc.).

berthing centre (n) Shipping term for department which performs similar tasks to a reservation section of an airline or tour operator. Also referred to as CBO.

B.E.V.A. (abbr.) British Exhibition Venues Association.

beverage (n) Any drink except water.

B.F.H.G.S. (abbr.) British Federation of Hotel Guest House & Self-Catering Association.

B.H.A. (abbr.) British Hospitality Association.

B.H.A.B. (abbr.) British Helicopter Advisory Board.

biosphere (n) The area in which life exists on the earth.

bilateral agreement (n) Agreement between two countries.

bill (n) Statement of money owed.

bird scarer (n) Member of staff whose job it is to keep birds away. If birds are sucked in to jet engines, they can do a large amount of damage and even cause accidents. Birds of prey are often flown to scare away smaller birds.

bistro (n) A small restaurant.

bisque (n) Fish soup.

BITOA (acr.) British Incoming Tour Operators Association.

black box (slang) The flight recorder on an aircraft. The flight recorder is actually in an orange coloured box for easy identification, this contains records of airspeed, altitude, direction, vertical acceleration and flight time. Some boxes also record everything that was spoken in the cockpit, thereby, providing a record to an accident investigator.

black economy (n) Black Market.

black excursion (n) An illegal excursion usually operated by Rep. without the com-

company's knowledge.

black frost/black ice (n) A coating of transparent ice, not readily visible; hence its danger to road users and on runways, as it can cause skidding.

black market (n) Illegal trading of goods.

black tie (n) Refers to bow tie worn with dinner jacket, but it now means that formal clothing is to be worn at function: dinner jacket for men and smart evening dress for women.

blizzard (n) Severe snow storm with high winds.

block booking (n) Reservation for more than one seat/room etc. booked at the same time.

block speed (n) The average speed in miles per hour of an aircraft between the time the aircraft first moves under its own power, until it comes to rest at the next landing point.

Blue Flag (n) Flag flown from a beach to denote that its cleanliness conforms to E.U. Bathing Water Directive standards.

Blue Badge (n) Term for British Registered Tour Guides.

board **1.** (v) To get on or into transport. **2.** (n) Food or meals provided.

boarding announcement (n) Instructions given by airline employees to inform passengers when aircraft are leaving and when passengers board.

boarding house (n) Small house providing inexpensive accommodation, generally owner managed.

boarding pass (n) Ticket given to passengers to show that they have checked in. This ticket is presented by passengers before getting on to transport.

boat drill (n) Practice of emergency procedure on a vessel at sea.

body (n) The main part of an aeroplane, cylindrical in shape. Also known as the fuselage.

body language (n) Recognisable process of communication by physical actions or positioning of the body, rather than by use of words.

bonded (n) Tour operator that has lodged a sum of money and/or insured against losses to protect clients interests.

bonding (n) System of insurance which ensures that clients' money is safe once they have paid for a holiday, even if the tour operator ceases to trade. Major associations such as ABTA, AITO, etc. operate a bonding scheme for their own members.

book (v) To order or reserve something in advance.

booked up (adj.) Fully booked, no places available.

booking agency (n) Company that reserves theatre tickets, hotel rooms, transport, etc. on behalf of a client.

booking form (n) Voucher or document used to confirm a reservation.

booking system (n) Method of recording clients payments and requirements for tours and services. These can be manual, on card, booking charts or by computer.

booth (n) Soundproof small room or structure where simultaneous interpreters work.

Bora (n) A cold wind blowing down from the mountains on to the Eastern Adriatic coast.

botel (n) Floating hotel.

boundary (n) Imaginary line marking the limits of an area of land, a geographical region, economies or societies.

bow/bows (n) Front or forward end of ship.

box office (n) Place at a cinema or theatre where tickets can be purchased.

brace (v) To stiffen one's body in preparation for a crash or an emergency landing.

brace position (n) Position of the body adopted to cause least injury when making an emergency landing.

breach of contract (n) Breaking a con-

breach of contract (n) Breaking a contracted agreement by not fulfilling all of the necessary terms and conditions.
break (n) **1.** Interval for refreshment. **2.** Short holiday.
break even (adj.) Amount of fare paying passengers needed to cover running costs of transport.
break out session (n) Small group discussions held during a larger meeting or conference.
breakdown (n) **1.** Mechanical failure of a vehicle. **2.** Period of time after an exhibition closes when stands are dismantled.
breakfast (n) First meal of the day.
bridge (n) **1.** Raised area on a ship from where the captain and crew control the vessel. **2.** A card game developed from whist.
bridle path (n) A path suitable for walkers and horses on which vehicles are not allowed.
briefing (n) Meeting to give instructions or information.
British Summer Time (n) National daylight saving time in the UK in summer, one hour in advance of Greenwich Mean Time.
broad/broads (n) A series of shallow, freshwater lakes linked by channels found in East Anglia: known as the Norfolk Broads.
Broadcasting Standards Council (org.) Statutory body that monitors advertisements that are broadcast on television and radio.
brochette (n) Food on a skewer.
brochure (n) Leaflet or booklet giving details of an operator's holidays, prices, terms and conditions etc..
Bronze Age (n) Period of time about 4,000 to 6,000 years ago, during this period bronze, an alloy of copper and tin, was used to make tools and implements.
brunch (n) Meal combining breakfast and lunch served mid-morning (US).
B.S.T. (abbr.) British Summer Time (UK).
B.T.A. (abbr.) British Tourist Authority.
B.T.C.V. (abbr.) British Trust for Conservation Volunteers. Voluntary organisation that offers holidays working on environmental projects (UK).
BTEC (acr.) Business and Technical Education Council. Now Edexel Foundation but still referred to as BTEC.
BUAC (acr.) British Universities Accommodation Consortium.
bucket and spade (n) A seaside holiday designed for children. Usually with sandy beaches so that children play in sand with a bucket and spade.
bucket shop (n) Company that sells tickets for air travel at very low prices.
budget **1.** (adj.) Inexpensive. **2.** (n) Estimate of money available and how it will be spent.
buffet (n) **1.** A selection of food provided, from which guests help themselves. **2.** A counter from which food is available at a station, on a train or ferry etc. (UK).
build up (n) A period of time before an exhibition or conference when staging and stand building takes place.
bulk clearance (n) When a group's luggage is cleared through customs together.
bulkhead (n) Dividing wall inside a ship or an aircraft.
Bullet Train (n) Japanese high speed train.
bumped (v) Off-loaded or denied a seat on an aircraft because of overbooking by the airline.
bunk (n) Bed built into a wall, or bulkhead, usually in a ship.
bureau (n) Information office or travel agency.
bureau de change (n) Office where currencies can be exchanged.
business class (n) Airline class - in

between Tourist Class and First Class designed to cater for the business traveller.
business house (n) Travel agency that deals only with business clients.
business lounge (n) See executive lounge.
business travel (adj.) Travel for the purposes of work.
butler (n) The person (traditionally a man) who is in charge of, the dining room, receiving visitors, and the other male staff in a large private house. Some luxury hotels now supply butlers with executive suites, they are responsible for the comfort of specific guests.
buying forward (v) When a company buys foreign currency in advance of requirements.
B.V.R.L.A. (abbr.) British Vehicle Rental & Leasing Association.

Cc - Charlie

C (abbr.) Business / Club class on an aircraft.
C. (abbr.) Symbol for Centigrade/Celsius.
C.A.A. (abbr.) Civil Aviation Authority.
C.A.B. (abbr.) Civil Aeronautics Board.
cab (n) Taxi.
cabana (n) American/South American term for a small changing room by the side of a swimming pool. A cabana can be booked/reserved for private use.
cabin (n) **1.** A room for sleeping and dressing on a ship. **2.** The seating area for passengers on an aircraft.
cabin attendant (n) A member of an airline's or ship's staff who looks after the passengers.
cabin crew (n) Staff who look after airline or ships' passengers. United Airlines was one of the first airlines to introduce cabin crew. Their area manager, Steve Simpson, had the idea of employing crew members to assist passengers, and in 1930 these crew started work - and the idea spread. Today cabin staff fulfil the dual role of safety and comfort of passengers.
cabin luggage/baggage (n) Small hand-held luggage that passengers are allowed to take with them onto the aircraft.
cabin pressure (n) Air pressure inside aircraft cabin.
cable car (n) A vehicle for taking people up steep mountains or hills. It is pulled and suspended from a moving wire cable.
cabotage (n) Air or sea traffic on routes within their own country's territory. These routes are not subject to international agreements on fares.
cafe complet (n) Continental breakfast with coffee.
cairn (n) A rough mound of stones piled up as a route marker, as a boundary indicator, or as a memorial.
call button (n) Switch which a passenger uses to call a cabin attendant.
camp (v) To stay or live for a short time in a tent which is out in the open air.
camper (n) **1.** A person who partakes in the act of camping. **2.** Short for camper van.
camper van (n) A vehicle in which people can eat and sleep.
camp-site (n) An area outside in the open that has space for tents.
canal (n) An artificial waterway that enables barges or boats to travel across land. Also used for irrigation.
cancel (v) Withdraw, annul, call off, discontinue. Cancellation (n)
cancellation charge (n) Payment levied when a ticket or service is cancelled.
canyon (n) A deep gorge/valley often with a stream or river.
capacity (n) The maximum amount allowed in a specific area, building or vehicle.

capital city (n) The most important town or city of a country or region due to the fact that it is usually the seat of government and the administrative centre.
capital works (n) large fixed investment that is usually associated with property (buildings) or equipment which is funded by long term loans or by the profits of companies or organisations.
captain (n) The person in charge of a ship or civil aircraft.
caravan (n) **1.** Mobile accommodation usually towed behind a car or horse. **2.** A covered motor vehicle equipped for living in (US). **3.** A group of pilgrims or merchants travelling together across a desert.
caravanserai (n) Place in Middle East where caravans, a collection of travellers usually with camels, stopped overnight. Now some have been turned into hotel accommodation.
Cardinal Points (n) The major points on a compass: North, East, South and West.
cargo (n) Freight or goods carried in the hold of an aircraft or by ship.
carnet (n) Official documentation or paperwork.
carousel (n) **1.** A rotating conveyor machine that sends the passengers' luggage around the arrivals hall of an airport for collection. **2.** Projector that has a slotted round drum situated on top that holds photographic slides.
carriage (n) **1.** The cost or the action of transporting or delivering goods. **2.** The separate long sections of a train that carry passengers (UK). In the US they are called cars.
carrier (n) Airline.
carry-on baggage (n) Hand-held luggage taken by passengers onto aircraft.
carrying capacity (n) The maximum number of people that a travel resort or attraction is able to sustain at any one time.
car sleeper train (n) Train carrying cars and with sleeping car couchettes or berths.
cartel (n) Informal agreement of companies to maintain prices at a high level and also to control marketing arrangements - i.e. airlines, hotel companies.
cartography (n) The study and production of maps and charts.
cash bar (n) A bar, usually found at private functions, where the guests have to pay for their drinks.
cash book (n) a book that is used to record all the transactions of an organisation - e.g. the money received from sales (receipts) and the money paid on out goings (payments).
cash flow (n) the flow of actual money in and out of a business.
casino (n) Room, building, or place used for gambling.
cassette (n) A small plastic box containing sound or video recording tape.
catchment area (n) Region that is covered by a service etc..
caterers (n) **1.** Company that provides food for events. **2.** Staff who cook and prepare meals.
catering (n) Providing food or meals.
cave (n) A natural hole underground.
C.B. (abbr.) Continental Breakfast.
C.C.P.R. (abbr.) Central Council for Physical Recreation.
C.C.T. (abbr.) Compulsory Competitive Tendering.
C.C.T.V. (abbr.) Closed Circuit Television (TV).
C.D.W. (abbr.) Collision Damage Waver. Agreement made when hiring a car. This means, in the event of an accident, the hirer guarantees to pay the initial amount of money towards repairs etc. before claiming insurance.
centigrade (n) A measurement of temperature. Freezing point of water is 0

degrees centigrade, boiling point of water is 100 degrees centigrade.

C.G.T.B. (abbr.) Canadian Government Travel Bureau.

C.H.A. (abbr.) Corporate Hospitality and Event Association.

chain (n) Group of hotels or shops that are owned or franchised by the same company.

chalet (n) **1.** Alpine house especially in Switzerland. **2.** A small house or hut on a beach or in a holiday camp.

chalet girl (n) A Young woman who looks after all the needs of guests staying in a chalet in a winter resort. Each day, the girl will clean the chalet, cook all the meals and generally look after the needs of the paying guests. She is usually employed by the tour operator who supplied the holiday to the guests, but some are employed privately by a specific family.

chambermaid (n) A woman who cleans and tidies bedrooms in a hotel.

channel (n) A natural or man-made watercourse.

charitable trust (n) a non profit making organisation that overseas the use of funds that are donated for the upkeep of property and assets.

chart (n) Specialised maps used by airline and ships' navigators.

charter (n) Aircraft wholly booked for a tour usually with no seats on sale to the general public.

chauffeur (n) Person employed drive people in a car or limousine.

cheapie (slang) Inexpensive ticket or tour.

check-in **1.** (v) Arriving at a hotel and going through the necessary procedures to stay in the hotel - i.e. collecting room keys. **2.** (v) Arriving at an airport and presenting your ticket etc. to enable you to board a flight. **3.** (n) Area in which check-in procedures take place.

check-out (v) Leaving accommodation - i.e. paying the hotel bill.

check-out time (n) Latest time for guests to vacate rooms. Guests who have not done so might be required to pay an extra charge depending on hotel policy.

checklist (n) Printed list used to check equipment is present or working correctly.

chef (n) Person who is responsible for the kitchen and cooking in a restaurant or hotel.

chef du parti (n) Chef responsible for the operation of the kitchen in a hotel or restaurant.

Chicago Convention (n) 1944 meeting which set up the ICAO. The Convention defines the five freedoms of the air, a list of types of Traffic Rights permitted under government agreement.

child minder (n) Person employed to look after children. See kiddies representative, nanny.

child seat (n) Small seat that is secured on top of a standard seat in transport so that children are safe while travelling.

Christmas (n) Christian Festival on December 25th each year. Celebrating the birth of Christ.

Chunnel (slang) Channel Tunnel - tunnel through which trains run providing a link between the UK and France.

chute (n) An inflatable rubber slide stored around the door of an aircraft for emergency evacuation.

CIF (acr.) Cost Insurance and Freight.

CIMTIG (acr.) Chartered Institute of Marketing Travel Industry Group.

C.I.P. (abbr.) Commercially Important Person/Passenger.

circa (preposition) About or approximately - usually refers to dates.

circle (n) Theatre or cinema seats in the lower balcony.

circle trips (n) Return journey, by a con-

continuous circular air route, not falling into the ordinary return or round-trip category.
circular tour (n) Tour starting and ending at the same point.
C.I.T. (abbr.) Chartered Institute of Transport.
citizen (n) A person who has the legal right to live in the particular country usually of their birth.
citizens (n) The people who live in a particular town or country. They do not necessarily have to be legal inhabitants.
citizenship (n) To have a legal right to live in a particular country.
C.I.T.O.G. (abbr.) Channel Island Tour Operators Group.
city breaks (n) Short holidays based in a city.
claim (v) Demand for money as compensation.
claim tag (n) Small ticket given by airline, as a receipt, when checking in luggage.
clearing (n) Leaving - i.e. Clearing Customs.
clearing house (n) An official or semi-official organisation which collects money, revenue and tickets and then distributes them to members.
Clefs d'or (n) Society of Golden Keys - International association of top Hall Porters.
clientele (n) A group of clients.
climate (n) Normal or average weather conditions in a particular area or country.
cloakroom (n) Place where coats etc. can be left.
closing stock (n) Value of stock that is held by a company or business at any period of time.
coach (n) A comfortable bus usually with only one deck (UK).
coach class (n) Economy Class (US).
coach control (n) Area where coaches wait at an airport or large venue.
coastal (n) Near or by the sea.
cockpit (n) Room or area from which an aircraft or small boat or yacht is controlled. See also flight deck.
cocktail lounge (n) Room or area where alcoholic drinks are served and where seating is provided.
C.O.D. (abbr.) Cash on Delivery
code of conduct/practice (n) Guidelines of the minimum standards for a group or association, which all members must follow or risk being asked to leave the group - i.e ABTA members have to adhere to the Association's Code, otherwise they are asked to leave.
code share (n) Alliance of different, sometimes competing airlines using the same airline prefix for agreed routes. Sometimes unpopular with passengers who do not know that they may not be flying on their preferred airline.
C.O.F. (abbr.) Coach Operators Federation.
coffee shop (n) Inexpensive restaurant/cafe in a hotel. Usually open throughout the day.
collision damage waiver (n) Extra insurance for car hire which covers the cost of the car if the driver is involved in an accident and does not affect the driver's own private insurance policy (i.e. loss of no claims bonus).
commentary (n) Talk given by Guide about a tour.
commercial delay (n) When airline check-in staff can ask for an aircraft's take-off slot to be delayed.
commission (n) Money paid to someone for selling goods or services after the sale has taken place and the amount of which depends on the amount of sales - i.e. the more sales made the more commission paid.
companion way (n) Stairs between the

decks of a ship.

compartment (n) Closed in seating area in a train.

compass (n) Device for showing direction - an instrument with a magnetic needle which points out due North.

compensation (n) Money or equivalent given to balance out or reduce the effect of services or goods that have not been satisfactory - i.e. a delay.

complain (v) To say that one is not satisfied with something.

complaint (n) Reason or statement that a customer is not satisfied with something.

complimentary (adj.) **1.** Given free of charge. **2.** Giving praise or compliments.

comply (v) To follow rules or instructions.

compulsory (adj.) Must be done or required by law.

Compulsory Competitive Tendering (n) A requirement of the Local Government Act 1988 setting up a process by which some local authority services, such as leisure provision, have to be defined in a contract for which private companies wishing to manage these services can complete.

concession (n) **1.** Reduction in price of tickets for particular groups of people - i.e. children or old age pensioners. **2.** A space or rented area within premises for running a small business or providing a service.

concierge (n) **1.** Hall Porter. **2.** Information desk clerk in hotel.

Concorde (n) **1.** Supersonic passenger plane. **2.** French hotel group.

concourse (n) A large open space in a public building, an airport, railway station, etc..

Conditions of Carriage (n) All carriers have detailed conditions of carriage which forms part of tickets. These conditions may alter the liability limits if the Warsaw or Athens Conventions.

condominium (n) An apartment block where each flat in the block is privately owned (US).

conference (n) Meeting of people for discussions or exchange of information, usually held on a regular basis.

confidential tariff (n) List of prices only given to travel agents and tour operators, not to the general public.

configuration (n) Aircraft cabin and seat layout.

confirm (v) To check or agree.

confirmation (n) Official agreement that something is correct or definite.

confirmed reservation (n) Booking that has been checked and the operator has agreed that there is a reservation.

congestion (n) Over-crowding with people, cars, aircraft etc..

congress (n) Large meeting or conference.

connecting flights (n) Two or more flights which in combination provide a journey from origin to required destinations.

connecting passenger (n) Traveller who does not have a direct flight to their destination and has to change aircraft during their journey.

connecting time (n) Minimum time for passenger arriving at an airport on one flight to catch next flight.

connection (n) When two transport services meet.

consecutive interpreting (n) Spoken translation of a speaker's words into another language, usually during a pause at the end of each sentence.

conservation (n) Protection of natural or man-made resources, including landscapes, buildings and their contents.

consolidate (v) Add together - i.e. two tours that have not sold well will be combined because individually they will not be profitable.

consolidator (n) Person or company that

excess capacity empty seats at lower than normal rates.

consortium (n) Group of independent companies or organisations that work together for a commercial or other advantage.

consul (n) Government official appointed to work and live in a foreign country to look after the interests of people from their own country travelling or living there. A consul can issue a new passport if one is stolen when abroad.

consulate (n) Official offices of the consul.

consultant (n) Professional advisor or expert.

consumer (n) Person who buys products or services.

Consumer Credit Act (n) Legislation which regulates the provision of credit (loans, hire purchase etc.) allowing people who have made a credit agreement a period of time during which they may cancel it. This safeguards against high pressure sales techniques.

consumer protection (n) Legislated legal protection for a person who purchases goods or services so that they actually get what they have paid for.

contingency plan (n) Plan preparing people to cope with possible but unpredictable events such as accidents or emergencies.

continental breakfast (n) Small breakfast usually Coffee, bread rolls, butter and jam.

continental plan (n) Accommodation that includes breakfast in the price.

contraband (n) Goods exported or imported illegally.

contract (n) Official legal agreement, usually written.

contractor (n) **1.** One of the parties to a contract. **2.** Person or company that is contracted to supply services.

controllable costs (n) Costs that can vary due to staff activity - i.e. private telephone calls, stationary. These costs can be controlled within the company - i.e. the stopping of private telephone calls and the prevention of stationary being used for private use.

conurbation (n) Marketing term for a heavily populated area where town boundaries merge.

convention (n) Conference (US).

co-pilot (n) The assistant pilot on an aircraft who is second in command to the captain. First officer.

corkage (n) Fee a restaurant/venue charges if you provide your own wine.

corporate image (n) Impression given by a company or organisation, this can be in the form of a logo or the impression of the company that is portrayed through advertising.

COSHH (acr.) Control Of Substances Hazardous to Health.

costing (v) Process of obtaining true costs, goods or services for accounting purposes.

cot (n) Small child or baby's bed.

COTAC (acr.) ABTA/City and Guilds Certificate of Travel Agency Competence.

COTAL (acr.) The Confederation of Latin American Tourist Organisations.

C.O.T.I.C.C. (abbr.) ABTA/City and Guilds Certificate of Tourist Information Centre Competence.

C.O.T.O.P. (abbr.) ABTA/City and Guilds Certificate of Tour Operating Practice.

C.O.T.O.R. (abbr.) ABTA/City and Guilds Certificate for Tour Operators' Representatives.

couchette (n) Small bunk or reclining seat on a train or a ferry designed for sleeping.

counter staff (n) Travel Agency booking clerk.

coupon (n) Ticket or voucher.

courier (n) A person who makes arrange-

Manager.

cover (n) **1.** Individual place setting at a table in a hotel or restaurant. **2.** The number of covers are the number of guests eating a meal at a function.

cover charge (n) Minimum charge added to a restaurant bill for service etc..

C.P. (abbr.) Continental Plan.

C.P.R. (abbr.) Cardiopulmonary Resuscitation. Emergency heart massage for first aid.

C.R.A.C. (abbr.) Continental Rail Agents Consortium.

crater (n) **1.** Large hole at the top of a volcano. **2.** Large hole in the ground caused by an explosion or impact of a large object, such as an aircraft.

creche (n) Children's nursery, where children are supervised and they can be left by their parents.

credit note (n) Given by a business to someone or somebody that it owes money to (creditor), this is usually done when goods supplied are faulty or unsatisfactory and is used as payment for future purchases.

creditor (n) Anybody or any person that an organisation or business owes money to.

crew (n) Members of staff on an aircraft or a ship/boat.

critical mass (n) To become financially viable an organisation must be able to achieve a minimum quantity sales, quality of product and range of products, these three requirements are called 'critical mass'.

Crown Classification Scheme (n) A voluntary scheme indicating the services and facilities available at a hotel/s.

CRS (abbr.) Computer Reservation System.

cruise (n) Holiday based on a ship.

C.S.A. (abbr.) Customer Service Agent - Airline receptionist.

C.S.Q. (abbr.) Customer Satisfaction Questionnaire.

C.T.C. (abbr.) Certified Travel Counsellor. Award of professional competence (US).

cultural tourism (n) Special interest tourism with art and historical tours.

culture shock (n) Cultural differences between countries or areas that cause travellers confusion.

currency (n) Official money of a country.

currency surcharge (n) The supplement added to any travel bill, as a result of exchange rate variations subsequent to the original cost calculation.

current assets (n) Anything owned by a business that can be sold and converts to cash in a short period of time - e.g. stock/shares.

current liabilities (n) Short term debt that is owed by a business or company - e.g. unpaid invoices, overdraft with the bank.

curriculum vitae (n) A written summary of a person's education, qualifications and career history.

customer (n) Person that buys goods or services.

customer records (n) Information that is held by an organisation with regard to their customers - e.g. address, buying habits.

customer satisfaction (n) when an organisation has fulfilled a customer's needs.

customer service (n) The elements of a organisation's business activities that relate to supplying the needs of the customer - these include areas such as efficiency, price, distribution and the handling of complaints.

customer service audit (n) A check carried out by an independent group which analyses in detail the quality of the service which a specific company is providing to customers.

customs (n) **1.** Officials, usually based at

a country's frontier, that are responsible for duty (tax) on taxable goods. **2.** traditional practices of a country or area.

customs hall (n) Area where passengers collect luggage and go through international entry procedures.

customs officer (n) Official who works in the Customs area.

customs pass (n) Daily Pass issued to non customs staff meeting a flight at an airport - i.e. issued to representatives of a tour operator.

customer profile (n) An evaluation of a typical customer using a particular service or buying a particular product.

cut off (n) Time at which hotel/venue will no longer hold a reservation.

cut-off date (n) **1.** Date when service finishes. **2.** Date after which something is no longer being sold - i.e. after the cut off date for a holiday no more bookings can be taken.

C.U.T.E. (abbr.) Common User Terminal Equipment.

C.V. (abbr.) Curriculum vitae

C.V.R. (abbr.) Cockpit Voice Recorder. See black box.

Dd - Delta

D. & D. (abbr.) Distress and Diversion (Air). Air traffic control sections for emergencies manned by Royal Air Force staff (UK).

"D" Train (n) German term for an express train (Durchgehende Zug).

dale (n) Name for a valley in Northern England (UK).

Danelaw (n) The areas of Northern England which were subject to Danish laws in the ninth and tenth centuries.

database (n) Information held on computer designed to be easily accessible. Usually comprising of basic information, lists of names and addresses, etc..

data protection (n) Ensuring that information stored on computer, usually personal, is not released to unauthorised persons or agencies.

Data Protection Act (n) Legislated act safe-guarding the privacy of the individual by regulating the use and storage of information about people on computer (UK).

dawn (n) The first light at the beginning of a day.

day delegate rate (n) Special price offered by hotels to conference organisers, which includes meeting room hire, coffee and tea, lunch, etc.. 24 hour delegate rate is all of this plus overnight accommodation, breakfast and dinner.

day hotel (n) Hotels built for short daytime stays often at airports or major stations.

day let (n) Bedroom in use during the day - e.g. for a meeting.

day visitor (n) A tourist who visits an attraction and does not make an overnight stay.

Daylight Saving Time (n) Time that is one hour later than standard time, generally used in the summer.

days of service (abbr.) Many services do not operate every day of the week. Days of service are designated by code numbers. Monday = 1; Tuesday = 2 and so on.

deadhead (n) **1.** Staff in transit travelling for free. **2.** Transport travelling empty for relocation or positioning.

deadline (n) The latest time for something. i.e. check-in.

debtors (n) Anybody or anyone whom owes a business or company money.

deck (n) The floor on transport such as boats/ships and buses.

deckchair (n) A folding chair that has canvas for the seat and also for the back. Commonly found on the beach (particularly UK), and on the decks of boats and

declaration (n) Written statement made to a customs officer giving details of goods being brought into a country.
deeds of covenant (n) A legal agreement during a set period of time that states the transfer of funds to another organisation or individual.
dehydration (n) Medical condition when the body has not taken in enough water to compensate for loss, through sweating, in a hot climate. Skin dehydration happens with air travel, where the skin dries out. Drinking water and using moisturiser helps to combat this.
delay (n) When transport or people cannot leave at the advertised time.
delegate (n) **1.** Attendee at a conference. **2.** Voting representative at an official meeting.
delegation (n) **1.** Assigning tasks or jobs. **2.** Group of delegates or officials.
delta (n) Low lying area at the mouth (exit into the sea) of a river formed by deposits of soil or alluvium (sand or clay gradually deposited on a river bed). Normally a 'D' shape when viewed from above.
de luxe (adj.) High quality or a high standard of comfort. Luxury.
demand (n) Desire for a product and the desire of a potential customer to pay for the product.
demarketing (adj.) When marketing of a product, resort or attraction is stopped to prevent people from visiting. This is done if the product etc. becomes too popular and marketing is not necessary or if the product etc. is being closed or stopped.
demi-pension (n) Hotel accommodation which includes bed, breakfast and one main meal per day.
demography (n) Characteristics of a population - e.g. income levels, age, population areas.
demonstration effect (n) Imitation of the behaviour and habits of customers.
demonstrator (n) Staff member, usually temporary, on an exhibition stand, who shows products to visitors.
denied boarding compensation (n) Payment by an airline to a passenger if they hold a guaranteed ticket and are unable to travel because the aircraft is overbooked.
density (n) The space available on a ship in relation to each passenger.
departure (n) The act of leaving.
departure lounge (n) Room in which passengers wait before boarding aircraft, ship etc..
departure tax (n) Tax payable before leaving a country.
deplane (v) To leave an aircraft.
deposit (n) Sum of money paid to secure a room, ticket or seat, normally this is only a small percentage of the whole value.
depreciation (n) The reduced monetary value of equipment over a period of time.
depressurisation (n) Emergency situation when the air pressure inside plane cabin drops rapidly.
depth markings (n) Numbering around a swimming pool showing the depth in feet or metres.
deregulation (n) Removal of trade restrictions or controls.
descent (n) Downward path of an aircraft.
desert (n) Dry barren area with little or no water or vegetation, normally sandy or with very poor soil.
dessert (n) Sweet course or pudding eaten at the end of a meal.
destination (n) Place to which something or somebody is travelling.
destination marketing (n) Promotion attracting visitors to a region, rather than a specific town or hotel.
determinants (n) The factors that effect potential customers' demands.

devaluation (n) To reduce the value of a currency in relation to other currencies.
dew pond (n) Generally a man-made pond or pool designed to collect and provide water.
D.G. XXIII (abbr.) European Commission department that deals with tourism.
diner (n) **1.** A person eating a meal in a restaurant. **2.** A cheap restaurant (US).
DINKY (acr.) Double Income No Kids. Term for couples that have no children and a large disposable income.
dinner (n) Main meal of the day. In the US, dinner is a main meal served in the early evening. In the UK dinner is any main meal served either midday or in the evening.
dinner jacket (n) Jacket worn, with a bow tie, by a man at formal social events. In the US this is called a tuxedo. When printed on an invitation it means men wear formal jackets and women long or very smart evening dresses.
diploma (n) Qualification obtained by examination or assessment.
diplomat (n) An official representing a country abroad.
diplomatic bag (n) Container in which documents and goods are dispatched to or from an embassy. Diplomatic bags are not usually subject to inspection by Customs.
directives (n) Instructions or rules set by an authority.
direct mail (n) The sending of promotional mail via the postal system by companies and organisations in order to promote the goods and services that they offer.
direct marketing (n) Marketing of goods and products on a personal basis without using a third party - e.g. direct mailing and telesales.
direct sell (n) Holidays sold directly to the public without using travel agents.
disco (n) Discotheque - A version of a night club usually associated with young people.
discount (n) Amount below the usual price - i.e. a deduction from a bill or the amount due.
discounted business/booking (adj.) Bookings or services given at a rate that is less expensive than the normal rate.
disease (n) Serious illness affecting a person or animal.
disembarkation (n) Leaving transport.
displacement effect (n) When one specific industry has the effect of taking financial resources and employment away from other industries.
disregard (v) 1. Take no notice, ignore. 2. Radio communication term that means the previous message or statement was incorrect.
district (n) An area of a town or country that has official boundaries for the purpose of official administration.
ditch (v) Make a forced landing or to intentionally bring an aircraft down on the sea in an emergency.
diversification (n) The broadening of a product range or range of services by a company - i.e. the creation of new services and products. This is usually done to protect the company from financial difficulties if one product starts to loose popularity.
diversion (n) When a vehicle/plane is rerouted.
D.M.C. (abbr.) Destination Management Company - i.e. company that organises events for tour groups at their place of arrival.
D.N.H. (abbr.) Department of National Heritage. UK Government Ministry that is responsible for Arts, Broadcasting, Film Industry, Millennium Fund, National Heritage, Sport and Tourism.
dock **1.** (n) An area of a harbour where ships and boats go to be loaded, unloaded and repaired. **2.** (v) When a ship is brought

into a dock.

document (n) Official paper or certificate.

documentation (n) All written paperwork that supports a business transaction.

Dollar (n) Unit of currency (Australia, N.Z., U.S. etc.) said to derive name from old Austrian coin, the Thaler.

Domesday Book (n) A survey of land and buildings in England carried out in 1086 by order of William 1 (William the Conqueror).

domestic (adj.) Internal flights or routes inside the same country.

domestic tourism (n) People taking holidays in their own country.

doorman (n) Uniformed member of staff on duty at the entrance of a hotel or grand venue, who opens car doors, shelters you with umbrella, etc..

double-decker (n) **1.** Bus/coach with an two floors for carrying passengers. 2. Two tier stand at an exhibition.

double occupancy (n) Two people sharing one bedroom.

dormitory (n) Room for sleeping in, containing a number of beds. Usually for young people.

D.o.T. (abbr.) **1.** Department of Transport (UK). **2.** Department of Transportation (US)

down market (n) Inexpensive or inferior.

downgrade (v) Move to less expensive or inferior seats or accommodation.

downtown (adj.) The centre of a town or city (US).

D.P.A.S. (abbr.) Document Printing and Accounting System.

draft (n) **1.** a rough or first copy of a document or proposal (see preliminary draft). **2.** A written money order (see bank draft).

drag (n) Air resistance on an aircraft or other vehicle.

draught (n) The depth of the bottom of a ship (the keel) below water.

driver (n) Person who drives a taxi, coach or other road vehicle.

drivers' hours (n) The legal length of time that a coach or bus driver is allowed to drive per day.

dry goods/stores (n) Tea, coffee, sugar and other powdered goods that will last for a long time.

dry hire (n) When equipment for an exhibition or Conference is hired without an operator.

dry lease (n) Where an aircraft is leased without an aircrew.

dual use (n) The use of a leisure facility for both educational and leisure use.

dupe (abbr.) Duplicate. Term used when there are too many passengers for a regular bus or coach service. This means that an additional coach or bus (dupe) will need to be provided in order to transport the additional passengers.

duplex (n) Hotel suite that has two floors that are connected by an internal stairway.

dusk (n) The time of the day when the light is disappearing, but it is not completely dark.

duty (n) **1.** Work schedule or roster - On Duty = working; Off Duty = not working. **2.** Tax on certain goods being brought into a country.

duty free (n) Goods that are sold free of taxes.

duty manager/officer (n) Manager/officer who is on duty or in charge at a certain time.

duty rota (n) Plan of staff working hours.

duvet (n) Bed cover filled with feathers, down, or foam, used in most European hotels.

D.W.B. (abbr.) Double With Bathroom. Double bedded room with an en-suite bathroom.

Ee - Echo

E (abbr.) Estimated.

E111 (n) Number of the form provided by Department of Health which entitles British nationals to free medical attention in countries that have arrangements with the British government (UK).

earphones (n) Covers or plugs for the ears which have small electronic speakers in them so that people can listen to sound without disturbing anybody else - i.e. for simultaneous translation or to listen to In-flight entertainment.

ear plugs (n) Pieces of soft foam which can be inserted in ear to keep out noise.

earthquake (n) A sudden violent movement of the Earth's surface, often causing great damage.

Easter (n) Annual Christian religious festival that takes place in March or April. Traditionally the start to European summer season.

E.A.T.A. (abbr.) East Asia Travel Association.

ebb (n) Water flowing away from the land - i.e. ebb tide.

E.C. (abbr.) European Community.

E.C.A.C. (abbr.) European Civil Aviation Conference.

eco- (prefix) Relating to protection of the environment - i.e. ecology, ecosystem.

ecology (n) Study of plants and animals in relation to each other and their natural environment.

economic impact (n) The positive and negative financial effects that an industry has on national and local communities.

economically developed (n) This usually refers to a country which has a high GNP by developing the primary, secondary and tertiary sectors of the economy.

economically developing (n) The process by which a country with a low GNP is developing and evolving by improving the primary, secondary and tertiary sectors of the economy - see economically developed.

economy class (n) Tourist class seats in an aircraft.

economies of scale (n) The ability of large purchasers to save money by negotiating lower rates than those placing smaller orders.

ecosystem (n) Collection of plants and animals that live within a particular physical environment.

eco-tourism (n) Tours that do not disturb the local environment whilst producing income for areas.

E.C.T.A.A. (abbr.) European Community Travel Agents and tour operators Association.

ECU (acr.) European Currency Unit.

educational trip (n) Organised visit where Travel Agents, Conference Organisers or the Press are invited to visit an area, a group of hotels, or place of interest. The object being to display the venues so that they will gain more business or publicity.

educational visit (n) Tour to a work place or factory which is topically relevant to a conference, etc..

E.F.A.H. (abbr.) European Foundation for the Accreditation of Hotel school programmes.

E.F.C.T. (abbr.) European Federation of Conference Towns.

E.F.T.A. (abbr.) European Free Trade Association currently comprises of many European countries that are not members of the E.U..

EH (abbr.) Eastern Hemisphere.

E.H.O. (abbr.) Environmental Health Officer. Official paid by local council to investigate health and safety matters in a borough or area.

E.I.A. (abbr.) Environmental Impact

Assessment. To measure the probable results of human intervention on the environment.

elapsed flying time (n) Actual time spent on a flight between two places.

elbow (n) Fare paid on transport to a crew member who keeps the payment.

electric supply (n) Socket or outlet from which electricity can be taken. This varies around the world - usually it is either 120 volts or 220/240. n.b. Never let travellers use the wrong plug or appliance for the local voltage as this can be dangerous.

electronic mail (n) Transfer of written information or images by means of computers linked by telephone to a central network.

electronic payment (n) Payment by means of electronic money transfer rather than cash or cheque.

electronic transfer of funds (n) The transfer of money from one bank account to another by computer.

elevator (n) **1.** See Lift (UK). **2.** Horizontal control surfaces on the wings of an aircraft used to control ascent and descent.

e-mail (n) See electronic mail.

embargo (n) Official ban on trade, this can include imports, flights or information.

embark (v) To go on board an aircraft or ship.

embarkation (n) Place or area at which a person embarks or leaves.

embarkation card (n) See boarding pass.

embassy (n) Official offices of the Ambassador in a foreign country.

emergency (n) A sudden serious situation or event that needs immediate action or attention.

emergency aid (n) First aid.

emergency card (n) Leaflet kept in the pocket of an aircraft seat, giving safety instructions.

emergency exit (n) Door designated as way out in the event of fire or any other emergency.

emergency landing (n) When an aircraft has to make a sudden, unplanned landing because of an emergency.

emigrant (n) A foreigner entering a country to take up permanent residence.

empty leg (n) Journey made with no passengers on board, usually when locating coaches or aircraft at the start or end of a tour or season.

empty nesters (n) A marketing term for potential clients whose children have left home.

empty run (n) See empty leg.

enclave/tourist enclave (n) When the tourists are isolated from the residents of the resort, this usually for the security of tourists.

endorsement (n) Official approval to support a claim, statement or course of action.

endowment (n) The money that is settled on a property that is used to maintain, restore and pay for it.

English breakfast (n) Cooked breakfast, with fried eggs, bacon and sausages etc..

English Channel (n) Stretch of water separating the United Kingdom from France.

en pension (n) Accommodation with meal/s.

enplane (v) To board an aircraft.

en suite (adj.) Accommodation that includes a private bathroom.

entrée (n) Food dish that forms main course of a meal.

entrepreneur (n) An individual that is prepared to take a financial risk by starting or creating a new business that has no guarantee of success.

environment (n) Surrounding area, especially an area in which people or animals live or work, respectively.

environmental audit (n) When a company or organisation looks at it's working meth-

or organisation looks at it's working methods and the effects these have on the environment.

environmental hazard (n) Natural danger - i.e. earthquake, flood, volcanic eruption or drought.

environmental impacts (n) Associated with the positive and negative effects of tourism - e.g. pollution.

environmentally sensitive area (n) Area with a fragile ecosystem which will only be maintained by conscious attempts to protect it.

E.P.O.S. (abbr.) Electronic Point of Sale.

E.P.S. (abbr.) European Passenger Services.

equator (n) Imaginary line around the centre of the world at an equal distance between the South and North Poles.

equatorial current (n) The surface movement of ocean currents near the equator.

equinox (n) One of the two days in the year when the day and night are of equal length. This normally happens around March 20 and September 20.

E.R.M. (abbr.) Exchange Rate Mechanism (European).

erosion (n) Gradual destruction of rock or soil by rain, wind, sea, ice.

escalator (n) A moving stairway/staircase that enables people to travel from one floor to another within a building or station.

escort (n) Courier, representative or companion.

escorted tours (n) Tours accompanied by a leader.

escrow (n) Arrangement where payment for a service or goods is held in a separate bank account or by an organisation not involved in the transaction. The payment is not transferred until the service or goods have been supplied.

E.S.I.T.O. (abbr.) Events Sector Industry Training Association.

estimate (n) Approximate calculation or amount.

estuary (n) Wide area of a river where it joins the sea.

E.T.A. (abbr.) Estimated Time of Arrival.

E.T.B. (abbr.) English Tourist Board.

E.T.D. (abbr.) Estimated Time of Departure.

ethnic traffic (n) Travellers from a particular racial group.

E-ticket (n) Electronic ticket issued from a machine operated by passenger.

E.T.O.A. (abbr.) European Tour Operators Association.

E.U. (abbr.) European Union. Political and economic association currently of fifteen European countries including, Austria, Belgium, Denmark, Finland, France, Germany, Greece, Holland, Ireland, Italy, Luxembourg, Portugal, Spain, Sweden and the United Kingdom.

EU Directive on Package Travel (n) European law that states the obligations required on tour operators to protect customers that have bought package holidays that includes two of the three elements, the three elements being travel, accommodation and services.

Euroline (org.) Company that runs a network of coach services across Europe.

european plan (n) Hotel rate for accommodation only, not including meals.

Eurostar (n) Train connecting the UK with France through the channel tunnel.

Eurotunnel (n) Tunnel under the English Channel joining France and the UK.

E.V.A. (abbr.) Exhibition Venues Association.

evacuate (v) To leave an area.

evacuation slide (n) Inflatable slide or chute, usually stored around door of an aircraft. The slide inflates in the event of an emergency, so people can use it to leave the aircraft quickly.

event (n) A planned social or public occasion.
event co-ordinator (n) Person who organises and oversees an event.
Everglades (n) Wetlands, with small islands, in Florida (US).
excess luggage (n) More luggage than allowed for in the ticket price. Usually carried at an extra charge.
exchange rate (n) Value of one currency compared to other currencies.
excursion (n) Short journey or visit made by people for pleasure.
excursion fare (n) Promotional fare offering a special low rate, often with a minimum or maximum stay requirement.
excursionist (n) Official term for a visitor to a country who stays for less than 24 hours.
executive cabin (n) Airlines passenger area adjacent to first class.
executive card (n) Card given by British Airways to identify the holder as a frequent traveller.
executive club (n) **1.** Private lounge at an airport reserved for V.I.P.s and business travellers of an airline. **2.** British Airways V.I.P. lounge.
executive lounge (n) A large room at airports and railway stations for specific travellers. These travellers could be guests of the airline, commercially important or members of an airline club.
exempt (adj.) Free from duty or payment.
ex gratia (adv.) Payment made by a tour operator to a client when a problem has arisen, this payment is made as a goodwill gesture, and not as an acceptance of blame or liability.
exhibition (n) Event or fair where companies or people display or show things.
exhibitors' pass (n) Identification card for people who have a stand at an exhibition in order to gain access to the exhibition.
exit (n) Way out.
expenditure (n) Money paid out or spent.
expenses (n) Money paid out to employees of an organisation to cover any costs that they incur while working - i.e. food and transport costs.
expiry date (n) Date after which something is no longer valid - i.e. a ticket.
export bureau (n) Office in a large shop or store that advises on the reclaiming of local taxes on goods purchased and also the shipping of goods purchased.
extend (v) Make longer or prolong i.e to stay on holiday longer than planned.
external business environment (n) Factors that can effect the operation and profitability of an organisation that are outside of its control- e.g. high level of local unemployment.
external checks (v) Checks a pilot makes before takeoff in an aircraft.
extras (n) Bill for items that are not included in the price, usually at a hotel.

Ff - Foxtrot

F (abbr.) **1.** First class. **2.** Symbol for Fahrenheit.
F.A.A. (abbr.) Federal Aviation Authority (US).
facility (n) Any item or any service provided at a venue to add to a visitor's pleasure or convenience.
facilitator (n) Person who makes something easier to do.
factory tourism (n) Where factories allow visitors to see how goods are manufactured.
Fahrenheit (n) A measurement of temperature. The freezing point of water is 32 degrees Fahrenheit, the boiling point of water is 212 degrees Fahrenheit.
fair (n) **1.** Large exhibition to promote business or visitors to a town or city. **2.** A

market or show with entertainments held regularly in the same venue, usually outdoors.

Fam. Trip (abbr.) Familiarisation Trip.

familiarisation trip/visit (n) A visit by a tour operator or a travel agent to a tourism facility that enables the operators and agents to experience the facilities so that they are able to best advise potential clients/tourists.

family cabin (n) Cabin with four or more berths.

Fantasia (n) C.R.S. for airlines including JAL and Qantas.

fare (n) The cost of travelling by transport from one destination to another.

farm tourism (n) Holiday where visitors stay on a working farm.

Far East (n) Referring to the countries of Eastern Asia including China, North and South Korea and Japan.

fast food (n) Hot food that can be purchased quickly and eaten in a shop or restaurant, and that can also be taken out and eaten whilst travelling or walking - e.g. fish and chips, hamburger, etc..

Fast Track (n) Initiative of B.A.A. to allow passengers that pay a premium through airport formalities quicker than other travellers.

Fastrak (acr.) CRS system used by tour operators.

fathom (n) Nautical measurement of depth. 1 fathom = 6 feet or approximately 2 metres.

fax (n) Facsimile machine. Machine that can transmit copies of letters, documents and illustrations electronically to other fax machines using telephone lines.

feedback (n) Comments from passengers or customers about products or services that they have used.

fens (n) Low lying wetlands in East Anglia (UK).

ferry (n) Boat or ship that carries people and/or vehicles across an area of water.

festival (n) Organised series of events, generally music, drama or dance performances taking place during a specific week or days.

F.I.A.V.E.T. (abbr.) Federazione Italiana del Associazioni Turistici.

field research (n) The research of a market in relation to products and services, this research is usually done by written and verbal questionnaires.

field trip (n) Journey made in order to study or research something in a practical way.

fiesta (n) Public holiday or celebration, especially a religious holiday.

filler (n) Short story or anecdote to fill in a pause during a commentary.

final approach (n) Last four miles of the approach to an airport by an aircraft during which time the aircraft is in a direct line with the runway for landing.

fine (n) Payment of money, as punishment for breaking the law.

fiord, fjord (n) A long narrow strip of the sea leading into the interior of a country.

fire exit (n) Way out or escape in the event of fire. By law these must be available in all public places, and must not be obstructed.

fire extinguisher (n) Canister containing water or chemicals which can be sprayed on a fire to put it out.

first aid (n) Medical attention or help given to an injured person before they are seen by a doctor or taken to a hospital.

first aid kit (n) See Medical Kit.

first class (n) Most expensive and the most comfortable area or cabins in a train, ship or aircraft.

first officer (n) Officer who is the assistant to the captain, usually second in command, on a ship or an aircraft. See also co-pilot.

F.I.S. (abbr.) Flight Information Service.

F.I.S. (abbr.) Flight Information Service.

fissure (n) A long deep crack in earth or rock.

F.I.T. (abbr.) Fully inclusive tour for Independent Travellers.

fixed assets (n) An asset that is always being used by a business or company - e.g. buildings.

fixed cost (n) The costs of a business or company that do not significantly change with fluctuating sales - e.g. rent.

flag (n) Piece of cloth which has a design or logo on it that represents a particular country or organisation.

flag carrier (n) National airline of a particular country.

flag of convenience (n) Flag of a country under which a ship registers, so that the owner of the ship can avoid paying the taxes or keeping to the regulations of their home country.

flaps (n) Moving parts on the wing of an aircraft to increase lift and/or drag.

flash flood (n) A sudden flood caused by heavy rain.

flexible (n) An arrangement or ticket that can be changed.

flight (n) Journey by air in an aircraft.

flight announcement (n) A notice given via a PA system on an aircraft.

flight attendant (n) Member of the cabin crew on an aircraft - see also air steward/stewardess.

flight coupon (n) Part of an air ticket used by a passenger to travel between points.

flight deck (n) Room or cabin at the front of an aircraft where the pilot and flight crew control the aircraft. Cockpit.

flight number (n) Official number given to a commercial flight. All flights travelling either north or east have even flight numbers; those travelling south or west have odd numbers - e.g. The flight London to New York is 001; from New York to London it is 002.

flight path (n) Course or direction of an aircraft through the air.

flight plan (n) Detailed form completed by aircraft captain before flight takes off, with information about the course, duration etc. of the intended flight.

flight series (n) Charter aircraft that are made available to a tour operator at a set time for a specific number of flights.

flipchart (n) Large sheets of paper fixed to a stand used to present information to an audience.

float (n) Money of small value notes and coins provided to someone before they start selling things so that they can give change.

floor (n) Level in hotel or building. In Europe at ground level is the ground floor and above that the first, second, etc.. In the USA the floor at ground level is the first floor.

floor plan (n) Map of the inside of a building being used as an exhibition, conference area etc. showing where each stand is located and also the location of other facilities.

floor show (n) Entertainment, a performance or an act in a bar or night club - i.e. dancers or singers.

flotilla sailing (n) Sailing holiday where holiday-makers sail and sleep on a group of yachts.

flow chart (n) Plan or timetable showing what tasks need to be done and in what order before completing an assignment or job.

FLT. (abbr.) Flight.

fly cruise (n) Holiday-makers travel by air to a sea port and then join a cruise ship.

fly-drive (n) Holiday which includes flying to a destination and car hire on arrival.

flyer (n) Single sheet leaflet used for advertising.

F.O.B. (abbr.) Free On Board. Cargo which is carried free.

F.O.C. (abbr.) Free Of Charge.

focusing (v) Identification of market segments in which an organisation is able to target their goods and services, this can be done by looking at the lifestyle or residential area of a potential customer.

foehn/föhn (n) A dry warm wind that occurs in Austria.

fog (n) Thick cloud of very small drops of water, or water vapour, in the air, which is difficult to see through.

food and beverage manager (n) Person in charge of food and drinks in a hotel, ship or conference venue, responsible for staff, finance and maintenance as well as supervising the serving of food and drink.

food court (n) Area where a number of different retail outlets provide and sell food.

food poisoning (n) Illness caused by eating food that contains harmful bacteria or chemicals.

footrest (n) Small bar or support usually underneath seat in front, for passengers to rest their feet on. Found on aircraft, coaches etc..

forced landing (n) Emergency landing by an aircraft.

foreign (adj.) Relating to or coming from a country that is not one's own.

foreign exchange (v) Changing money from one country's currency into another.

forest (n) Large area of land covered with trees.

formalities (n) Official rules or procedures - i.e. to show your boarding pass and passport when boarding an aircraft.

forward **1.** (adj.) Front section of the ship. **2.** (v) To send mail to forwarding address.

forwarding address (n) New address given when leaving accommodation to which mail should be sent to.

fossil (n) Hardened remains of a plant or an animal found inside rock.

four poster bed (n) Bed with four posts at the corners which hold up a canopy.

foyer (n) Hall or lobby of a hotel or venue.

Franc (n) Unit of currency - in France, Belgium etc..

franchise (n) Authority given by a company or organisation to someone allowing them to sell its goods or services or run a business to do the same using the original organisations name.

freehold (n) A property that is able to be passed/sold by the owner to a third party which is also not attached to a lease.

free house (n) Pub (Public house) that sells beers from several breweries and is not owned by one brewery (UK).

free luggage (n) Allowance for luggage carried free. Also referred to as Baggage Allowance.

free port (n) Area of a port, where duties or taxes are not paid, often because the goods will be re-exported.

freebie (slang) Journey, entrance, service or goods provided at no cost.

Freesale (n) System whereby reservations can be confirmed immediately to a client.

freeway (n) Multi-lane road (US).

frequency (n) The number of times a service occurs in a certain period - i.e. train timetables tell you of the frequency of trains.

frequent flyer (n) Those who travel regularly with an airline and are often rewarded with gifts or vouchers as an incentive.

fringe meeting (n) Gathering at a conference for delegates to discuss subjects not directly related to the subject of the main conference.

frisk (n) To search a person by hand to find out if they have concealed weapons, drugs or other illegal items.

front office (n) Office responsible for the

administration of a hotel reception.
front of house (n) Reception area of a hotel.
frontier (n) The area or border between one country and another country.
F.T.O. (abbr.) Federation of Tour Operators.
full 1. (n) A ticket of the maximum or adult price. **2.** (adj.) Complete, or with nothing available - i.e. transport with no empty seats.
full board/pension (n) Accommodation that includes three meals a day.
function (n) Formal ceremony or meal.
function sheet (n) List giving details of events to be held at a venue.
fuselage (n) See body.

Gg - Golf

gala dinner (n) Principal social event, especially at conference or end of a luxury tour.
gale (n) Wind speed above 100 k.p.h..
Galileo (n) C.R.S. for airlines including BA, Alitalia, Swissair, Olympic & KLM.
gallery (n) **1.** Place where art is on display. **2.** Indoor balcony in large room or theatre.
galley (n) Kitchen on boat, ship or aircraft.
game lodge (n) Accommodation in safari parks.
game reserve (n) Conservation area where visitors can see wild animals in their natural habitat.
gangway (n) **1.** Passageway between rows of seats. **2.** Movable platform or bridge, placed between a ship and the shore, allowing people to embark and disembark.
gate (n) Exit in an airport departure lounge that leads to the aircraft.
gateway (n) **1.** Main airport or port of entry to a country. **2.** City which forms the entrance of a geographical area.
G.B.C.O. (abbr.) Guild of British Coach Operators.
G.B.P. (abbr.) Great Britain Pound.
G.B.T.A. (abbr.) Guild of Business Travel Agents.
general sales agent (n) Agent appointed by company to act as principal or sole agent to sell services, tickets or accommodation.
geographical location (n) Market segmentation that classifies customers into areas of residence.
geyser (n) Natural hot water spout or spring that sends water up from the ground.
G.F.I. (abbr.) Green Flag International. Association encouraging ecological awareness amongst tour operators.
G.I.T. (abbr.) Group Inclusive Tour.
gîte (n) Self-catering cottage (Fr.).
glacier (n) A mass of ice, which moves, extremely slowly, sometimes through a mountain valley.
glen (n) A narrow, steep-sided valley in Scotland (UK).
globalisation (n) The process during which a company, product, or service becomes totally international e.g McDonalds is present in many countries and is said to be global.
gluwein (n) Spicy hot red wine drink popular in the European Alps.
G.M.T. (abbr.) Greenwich Mean Time. Usually shown by 'Z' written after the time.
GNVQ (abbr.) General National Vocational Qualification
G.N.P. (abbr.) Gross National Product.
gondola (n) **1.** A narrow boat with a flat bottom that is particularly used in Venice (Italy) as a method of transport. **2.** A small cable car.
gods (n) Gallery seats in highest part of theatre.

goodies bag (n) Amenity Kit.
gorge (n) A deep and narrow valley, or opening in the earth, usually containing a river.
go technical (slang) When an aircraft becomes unserviceable.
G.P.C.A. (abbr.) Guild of Professional Cruise Agents.
G.P.S. (abbr.) Global Positioning System. System which helps aircraft and ships find their current location.
G.P.W.S. (abbr.) Ground Proximity Warning System.
grand circle (n) Theatre seats on the first floor - usually with the best view.
grandstand (n) Large structure with rows of seats for spectators at sporting events.
gratis (adj.) Free.
grats. (abbr.) Gratuities.
gratuity (n) Tip, extra payment for a service.
green belt (n) An area of land around a large town or city where new development is strictly controlled.
green card (n) **1.** Insurance certificate needed by drivers of cars, when travelling out of their home country. **2.** Work permit for foreign nationals in the US.
Green Flag (org.) Car Rescue Service.
Green Flag International (org.) Non-profit making conservation company, which works in conjunction with the tourism industry to improve the environment.
Green Globe (n) Worldwide environmental management and awareness programme for the Travel & Tourism Industry, open to companies of any size, type and location, committed to improvements in environmental practice.
green tourism (n) Tourism that tries to sustain, improve or protect the environment.
grid reference (n) To find places easily on a map. The map is split into squares and divided by lines which are numbered or lettered. To locate any point on the map a note is made where these lines intersect or cross.
grockle (slang) Word for tourist, originated from the county of Cornwall (UK).
Gross National Product (n) The total value of the goods and services produced by a country that includes the country's investments and income from any assets overseas.
Gross Profit (n) Difference between the cost and the selling price of an item or product (excluding VAT).
Gross Profit Margin (n) The percentage of profit in relation to the selling price (excluding VAT).
ground arrangements (n) Local services provided for visitors at their destination.
ground handler (n) **1.** Company that supplies services at a destination on behalf of a tour operator - i.e. meet and greet, check-ins, sightseeing etc.. **2.** Company that supplies passenger handling services on behalf of an airline.
ground services (n) Division of an airline that handles all the activities of an airline at an airport.
group (n) Collection of people, passengers or clients.
G.S. (abbr.) General Sales agent.
G.S.A. (abbr.) General Sales Agent.
guard (n) **1.** Official in charge of passengers on a train. **2.** Official steward in a museum.
guarantee for late arrival (n) Hotel accommodation held all night with guarantee of payment for non/late arrival of guests.
guaranteed payment reservation (n) A hotel booking, made on the understanding that should, for any reason, the client not arrive, the travel company will be responsible for payment.
guest (n) Client or visitor staying in hotel

or similar accommodation.

guest house (n) Small establishment, often run by a family, that provides rented rooms for accommodation.

guest services (n) Facilities provided for the enjoyment of clients - i.e. gym, restaurants, bars, library, etc..

guest services manager (n) Person in charge of seeing that clients enjoy their stay at a hotel or resort - e.g. by organising excursions, sports and showing guests to facilities and introducing guests to each other.

guide (n) Person who leads a visit or tour. A guide shows and explains local history, geography and life of a region, city or town.

guide book (n) Book, designed for tourists, giving details of history, architecture and general features of an area, town, city or country.

guided tour (n) Tour or visit led by a guide.

Guild of Sommeliers (n) International association, to which many of the top wine waiters are members.

Guilder (n) Dutch unit of currency.

gulf (n) A large inlet from the sea.

Gulf States (n) Countries in the Middle East located around the Persian Gulf.

Hh - Hotel

half board (adj.) Accommodation including only breakfast and one main meal, normally the evening meal.

half day (adj.) Tour or event taking half a day to complete.

hall porter (n) Member of hotel staff in charge of luggage, messages, information etc.. Also known as a concierge.

hamlet (n) **1.** A very small village or settlement, often without church or shops. **2.** The mild cigar.

handicapped (adj.) Person who has a physical or mental disability.

hand luggage (n) Luggage or baggage carried by passengers onto a coach or an aircraft.

handling fee (n) Amount charged by agent for local arrangements.

hand outs (n) Forms, leaflets, information sheets etc. which are given out free to visitors, telling them more about a service, site, building or company.

harbour (n) A small and normally well sheltered sea port.

hard currency (n) National currency which is stable and unlikely to suddenly lose its value against the currencies of other countries. e.g. US dollars, UK Sterling.

hatch (n) An opening or a door in the deck of ship or in the body of an aircraft.

H.A.T.T.A. (abbr.) Hellenic (Greek) Association of Travel and Tourist Agencies.

haul (n) Part or leg of a journey - i.e. Short Haul = short distance; long haul = long distance.

haute cuisine (n) Cookery of a high standard (Fr.).

hazard (n) Anything that is a risk or danger.

H.C.I.M.A. (abbr.) Hotel Catering and Institutional Management Association.

head count (n) The number of passengers on a coach, in a boat etc..

headland (n) High narrow section of land that forms a point out into the sea.

headrest cover (n) Cover, usually washable cloth, which protects the top of a seat from dirt.

head wind (n) Wind blowing from in front of an aircraft, boat or other vehicle pushing it backwards and making it travel more slowly.

health club (n) Area in a hotel or apartments that contains fitness equipment, gym and usually a swimming pool.

Health and Safety Act (n) Act of Parliament specifying the requirements of an organisation to ensure that there are no dangers or hazards to the employees or customers (UK).
health and safety equipment (n) The items or equipment to implement health and safety - e.g. fire extinguishers in the workplace, first aid equipment and safety labels on products.
health and safety hazards (n) Potential dangers that could threaten life or cause injury - e.g. blocked fire exits.
heatstroke (n) See sunstroke.
hectare (n) Metric measurement of land area 10,000 square metres. 1 Hectare = approx. 2.5 acres.
helicopter (n) Type of aircraft with an engine that powers overhead revolving blades (rotors) to give lift and flying capability.
helipad (n) Landing space for helicopters.
heliport (n) Airport for helicopters only.
help yourself (adj.) Self-service.
heritage (n) Relics of a country's past or history, handed down from one generation to the next.
heritage tourism (n) Tourism that is only concerned with historical sites.
H.H.A. (abbr.) Historic Houses Association.
high season (n) The time of year when most people take holidays, this usually coincides with the summer months.
high tide (n) The time of the day when the sea level is highest - See tide.
hijack (v) To take control illegally of an aircraft or other form of transport.
hiker (n) Person who travels by walking.
hill fort (n) Fortified site on top of a natural hill.
hire (v) Rent or charter.
hitch hike (v) Travel by getting free rides in other peoples' vehicles. If a coach picks up a hitch-hiker it will usually invalidate any insurance that the coach has.
hold (n) Place on an aircraft or ship where luggage and freight is stored while in transit.
holding (n) When aircraft have to wait in the air for landing clearance when approaching an airport.
holiday (n) Time during which people relax or enjoy themselves while away from work. This may include travelling for pleasure or other leisure time activities. Vacation.
holiday camp (n) Place that provides accommodation and entertainment for large numbers of people (UK).
holiday maker (n) Person who is on holiday, usually away from home.
home exchange (n) Scheme where two home owners who swap their home with others for a temporarily for a holiday. People wishing to do this can join an agency for a fee. They then receive a list of others who want to do the same and it is up to them to contact these home owners and exchange occupancy of their homes for their holidays.
honeymoon (n) Traditional holiday taken by a couple just after they are married.
honeypot (adj.) Well-known destination or venue that is generally over-crowded during high season.
horizon (n) The line that is seen from far distance where the sky seems to meet the sea or land.
horizontal integration (n) When two companies at the same level of business merge with another to create a larger company that continues in the same business activities - e.g. one travel agency merging with another.
hors d'oeuvre (n) See starter.
hospitality desk (n) An information desk usually for a particular group's use.
hospitality room (n) Room set aside for a

hospitality room (n) Room set aside for a particular group.
host (n) Man who looks after passengers or delegates.
host community (n) Refers to the inhabitants of an area/community where tourists visit - i.e. what effect do the tourists have on the daily lives of the inhabitants. See environmental impact.
hostel (n) Inexpensive hotel accommodation often with shared rooms.
hostess (n) Woman who looks after passengers or delegates.
hot air balloon (n) Large balloon filled with heated air causing it to float through the air. A basket hangs from the balloon for people to travel in.
hot connection (n) When minimum connecting time for transit passengers is inside time allowed.
hotel (n) Accommodation where people pay to stay.
hotel garni (n) Hotel that provides a limited catering service to guests.
hotel manager (n) Senior management job in a hotel, responsible for the running and financial success.
hotel register (n) Record of hotel guests.
hotel voucher (n) Ticket or document used to confirm that a client has prepaid for a hotel room.
house guide (n) Person working in a stately home, house etc. who conducts tours around the property.
housekeeper (n) Person in charge of bedrooms in a hotel.
hovercraft (n) Transport that is similar to a boat that rides on cushion of air. It can travel on land as well as water - invented by Sir Christopher Cockerill.
hub (n) Base or home port for an airline, into which it flies from other airports and passengers connect with other aircraft of the airline and fly to further destinations.
hub and spoke (n) Feeder services from small airports that are linked to services flying to other destinations.
hull (n) The main body of a boat, ship, yacht, cruise liner etc..
human resources department (n) Personnel department.
humid (adj.) Climate which is hot and damp. Generally very uncomfortable.
hurricane (n) Violent wind or storm, With wind speeds over 140 k.p.h..
hydro-electricity (n) Energy produced by taking power from mountain streams and rivers by damming their output.
hydrofoil (n) Boat that rides up on skis when travelling at speed.

Ii - India

I.A.C.V.B. (abbr.) International Association of Convention and Visitors' Bureaux.
I.A.P.C.O. (abbr.) International Association of Professional Congress Organisers.
IATA (acr.) International Air Transport Association.
I.A.T.M. (abbr.) International Association Tour Managers.
I.C.A.O. (abbr.) International Civil Aviation Organisation. Governing body for air safety, communication etc..
I.C.C.A. (abbr.) International Congress and Convention Association.
iceberg (n) A large mass of ice that floats in the sea. Can be a danger shipping.
I.C.O. (abbr.) Independent Conference Organiser.
i.d. card/pass (n) Official identification pass - e.g. pass used to enter a security zone.
identikit destination (n) Tourist resort that copies the features of a destination that already attracts large numbers of

Permit carried by car drivers that enables them to drive in a country outside their own.

I.F.A.L.P.A. (abbr.) International Federation of Air Line Pilots' Associations.

I.F.E. (abbr.) In-Flight Entertainment.

I.F.T.O. (abbr.) International Federation of Tour Operators.

I.F.W.T.O. (abbr.) International Federation of Women's Travel Organisations.

I.H.E.I. (abbr.) International Hotels Environment Initiative.

I.I.T. (abbr.) Independent Inclusive Tours.

I.L.S. (abbr.) Instrument Landing System. Equipment used at night or in bad weather to help the pilot of an aircraft during final approach and landing.

immigration (n) Official point on arrival in a country where identification and entry visas of passengers are checked.

immunisation (n) Vaccination against disease. See also vaccination.

impact (n) Collision or crash.

implant (n) When a travel agency puts a member of their own staff in a client company to handle bookings etc. - usually because the client company does a large amount of business with the travel agent.

imprint (n) The mark made by imprinting details on a bill or voucher using a machine.

inaugural flight (n) First flight on an airway route or the first flight of a new aircraft.

inbound (n) Transport or passengers coming into a country or area.

inbound tour operators (n) tour operators that provide holidays for tourists visiting the native country of the tour operator.

INCAD (abbr.) Incapacitated Passenger Handling Document. Form used when a passenger needs a wheelchair.

incentive (n) Prize or award offered to encourage business or to motivate staff.

incentive travel (n) Specialised section of the industry that handles incentive travel trips.

inclusive (adj.) Items that are included in a set price or cost - i.e. accommodation with meals.

inclusive cost (n) One-off payment with no extra charges or fees added at a later time.

inclusive holiday/tour (n) Holiday package with everything included in the price.

Inclusive Tour by Charter (n) A package holiday when the travel consists of a charter flight.

Inclusive Tour by Excursion (n) A package holiday where the travel consists of a scheduled flight.

incoming (n) Transport or passengers arriving in a country or area.

Independent Inclusive Tours (n) Package holidays that are produced and sold by travel agents using commission rates from principals in hotels and transport.

independent travel (n) Travel that is undertaken by a person who makes his/her own arrangements for transport and accommodation.

induction (n) Introductory talk to new employees, visitors etc..

induction loop (n) Closed circuit wire within a building which relays sound to a hearing aid or a simultaneous translation receiver.

industrial revolution (n) Introduction of mechanical methods of producing goods and also of large scale factories. This started in the UK at the end of the 18th century.

infant (n) Child under two years old.

inflation (n) General rise in the cost of goods and services within a country causing money to decrease in real value. When this happens it can mean that country's currency is lose value against other currencies.

in-flight (n) Taking place during a journey by air.
in-flight catering (n) Food and drink provided during a flight on an aircraft.
in-flight entertainment (n) Anything offered by an airline to keep passengers entertained during a journey by air - i.e. films, videos, tapes, gambling etc..
information (n) Facts or knowledge.
information board (n) Notice board used by representatives to display notices about excursions, departure times and other resort information.
infrastructure (n) The basic necessities needed to operate a town, city or resort - i.e. sewage, lighting, water supply, roads and transport.
inhabitant (n) Person living in an area, town, city or country.
in-house (n) Services organised within hotel or company - i.e. in-house catering at a conference venue.
inn (n) Small pub or hotel.
innovation (n) The creative development of new products.
inoculation (n) See vaccination.
inside cabin (n) Room on ship without a porthole or window.
insurance (n) Contract whereby the insurer guarantees that a certain sum will be paid for a specified loss, injury or accident.
intangible / intangible assets / intangible **benefits** (n) Assets and benefits that cannot be seen but can be experienced.
integrated resort (n) A resort that has all the facilities on one site - e.g. restaurants, transport, entertainment and accommodation.
interaction (n) When people come together and react to each other. This is often encouraged at special sessions at conferences, when people work together in small groups to produce a reaction that will bring out new ideas.
interline (n) Connections between different airlines.
interlining (n) When passengers make a journey transferring between different airlines while using only one ticket.
internal business environment (n) The factors that an organisation or a company can effect directly - i.e. employees, suppliers, customers.
international date line (n) An imaginary line that approximately follows 180° longitude. People travelling east to west over this line gain an extra day. Travellers from west to east lose a day.
international money order (n) Bank draft drawn in the currency of the receiving country - e.g. A US dollar invoice can be paid with a dollar money order drawn on a UK bank.
Interpol (n) International Police agency.
interpreter (n) Person who translates verbally from one language to another.
interpretation centre (n) Office or facility giving an explanation of a site of interest, nature reserve, etc..
interview (n) A meeting between a potential employee and a employer to see if the potential employee is suitable for a job vacancy.
in transit (adj.) **1.** People or goods that are currently travelling. **2.** When passengers lay over or stay in a country that is not their final destination usually without leaving airside or customs area of an airport.
inventory (n) A list of stock or contents.
investment (n) The process of spending money or time to try and get a greater return. i.e. If a company spends money on advertising they are trying to get business which will return more money than they have spent (make a profit).
invisibles/invisible assets (n) Income received by a country trading in services rather than goods. Invisible assets include

tourism, banking, shipping and investments. Goods are counted as visible assets.

invitation (n) Request to attend a function.

invoice (n) List of goods or services supplied, including their prices. Bill.

I.O.J. (abbr.) Institute Of Journalists.

I.O.L. (abbr.) Institute Of Linguists.

Iron Age (n) Historical period after the Bronze Age when iron started to be used to make tools and weapons. Approximately 500 BC.

irrigation (n) Method of supplying water to land or crops by means of channels or pipes.

island (n) **1.** Area of land completely surrounded by water. **2.** Check-in desks isolated on concourse rather than in a line.

Istel (n) CRS system used by tour operators.

isthmus (n) A narrow strip of land surrounded by sea, connecting two larger areas of land.

I.T. (abbr.) **1.** Inclusive Tour. **2.** Information Technology.

I.T.A.A. (abbr.) Irish Travel Agents Association.

I.T.C. (abbr.) Inclusive Tours by Charter.

itemised account (n) A statement that shows every single transaction between an organisation and a customer.

itinerary (n) Detailed description, record or plan of a visit, tour, journey or route.

I.T.M.A. (abbr.) Incentive Travel and Meetings Association.

I.T.T. (abbr.) Institute of Travel and Tourism.

I.T.X. (abbr.) Inclusive Tour excursions - usually applied to an airfare.

Jj - Juliet

J (abbr.) Business class on airlines

J.A.A. (abbr.) Joint Aviation Authority.

Jacuzzi (n) Large warm bath with jets of water - often communal.

jet (n) Aircraft propelled by jet engines.

jet lag (n) A feeling of tiredness and confusion after a long journey by air, normally when passengers travel between time zones.

jet stream (n) Strong wind that blows in the atmosphere.

jetfoil (n) Fast boat that rides up on skis while at speed. A hydrofoil is similar.

jetliner (n) Airliner (US).

jetty (n) **1.** Small pier projecting into water. **2.** Airbridge. Movable corridor brought to the doors of an aircraft to allow people to exit and to enter from the airport.

JICTOURS (acr.) Joint Industry Committee for Tourism.

job description (n) The details of the responsibilities/standards required by an employer from an employee.

joining instructions (n) Letter sent to passengers or delegates confirming details of travel arrangements, including times and dates.

journey (n) Travelling from one place to another.

jumbo jet (slang) Boeing 747.

jump seat (n) Crew seat in an aircraft that retracts (jumps) back against a bulkhead, for storage, when not in use.

Kk - Kilo

keep (n) Area of a castle, usually a tower in the middle of the castle, that was easy to guard and defend, where the food and stores were kept in the event of a siege.

key card (n) Small plastic card with a magnetic strip, similar to a credit card, used for security reasons instead of keys for hotel rooms and ships' cabins.

keynote speech (n) Important speech setting the theme of a meeting or conference.

kiddies representative (slang) Person

employed to look after children on holiday - to allow parents to undertake activities without them. See nanny and child minder.
kilometre (n) Metric unit of distance. One kilometre = 1,000 metres or 0.62 miles.
king size bed (n) Large double bed.
kiosk (n) **1.** Small box-like structure from which tickets, programmes etc. can be purchased. **2.** Small shop or concession selling newspapers, cigarettes etc.. See concession and box office.
kitchen porter (n) The most junior position/job in a kitchen, involving washing-up and vegetable preparation. Also known as a plongeur.
knee biters (slang) Children, used in museums and tourist venues.
knock on effect (n) When an initial action or event causes several other actions or events to happen - i.e. If oil prices increase, it has a knock-on effect on transport costs and therefore holiday pricing.
knot (n) Nautical measurement of one nautical mile per hour.
K.P.H. (abbr.) Kilometres Per Hour.

Ll - Lima

labour-intensive (n) When a company requires a larger than usual workforce in order to undertake business and services - i.e. a catering company has to employ many waiters and waitresses when undertaking a catering contract.
L.A.I. (abbr.) Local Area Initiative - partnership set up between the Tourist Boards, Local Authorities, other agencies and private firms with clearly defined objectives. Programmes agreed between partners usually run for a three year term.
land **1.** (n) An area of ground. **2.** (v) When an aircraft or ship arrives after a journey.
landfall (n) The first sight of land after a voyage by sea.
landing (v) When an aircraft touches down on runway after flight.
landing card (n) Form filled in by passengers and handed to the immigration on arrival in a country.
landmark (n) A particular physical feature of a location that can be easily recognised by travellers, in order to judge their position. e.g. A prominent hill or tower.
landscape (n) Geographical area that has a distinctive appearance when looking across it. It can be natural or man-made.
landscape architect (n) Designer of gardens, parks and plants and trees. Probably the most famous was 'Capability' Brown, who redesigned the park lands surrounding stately homes such as Blenheim Palace and Stowe School. He was known as 'Capability' because of his frequent comments that an area had capabilities.
landside (n) Area at airport before passengers go in to Customs or Airside.
langlauf (n) Cross country skiing particularly popular in Scandinavia. Also known as Nordic skiing.
lapel mike (n) Small microphone that can be clipped onto a person's clothes.
L.A.T.A. (abbr.) Latin American Travel Association.
late bookings (n) Bookings made at the last time possible, sometimes with extra charges or discounts.
late check-out/late departure (n) When hotel guests have arranged to leave after normal check-out time.
Latin America (n) Central and South America.
latitude (n) Distance measured in degrees, north or south from the equator.
layover (n) **1.** Compulsory stop, usually overnight, for aircrew who otherwise would be working more than their permitted hours. **2.** When passengers break a journey due to lack of connecting flights.

journey due to lack of connecting flights.
L.C.O. (abbr.) Lowest Cost Operator.
lead name (n) The name of the first person on a booking form, this person should be over eighteen years of age and should sign the booking form.
leakage (n) Any factor which causes profits from tourism to be taken away from the place where the tourism occurs.
lease (v) Rent or hire - usually applied to capital items such as aircraft, cars boats or property.
lectern (n) Small high table with angled top on which a speaker or lecturer can put their script or reference material and read from it while speaking to an audience.
leg (n) Section of a journey.
legacy (n) Money or property that is left in a will.
leisure (n) Free time that is used for enjoyment.
leisure activity (n) Sport or recreational activity that is carried out in the time that a person is away from work.
leisure card (n) Card given by some UK local authorities to local residents, entitling them to free or reduced price use of leisure amenities/facilities.
leisure day visitor (n) Someone who visits an attraction or venue for one day only - i.e. a theme park or stately home.
leisure industry (n) Companies providing the means, facilities and equipment for people to utilise their leisure time.
leisure time (n) Time away from work or other duties in which recreational activities etc. can be done.
Le Shuttle (n) Trade name for the channel tunnel car and passenger carrying train service between the UK and France.
lessee (n) Client that rents space in a building or in a conference venue.
lessor (n) Official working on behalf of the owners of a building or a conference venue that rents out space or facilities.
let down (v) When the wheels or undercarriage of an aircraft are lowered into position, ready for landing.
letter of application (n) A letter that is sent to a company or organisation with reference to a job vacancy, this letter will usually accompany a curriculum vitae (CV).
liable (adj.) When a company has a legal responsibility for something.
liability (n) The maximum amount compensation (money) for which a company or organisation is responsible for something.
licence (n) Formal or legal permission to operate something, carry out a service or drive a vehicle.
licensed (n) Bar or place which can serve alcohol.
licensee (n) The person to whom the authorities have granted permission to sell alcohol on specified premises.
life jacket (n) Inflatable or buoyant clothing which keeps a person afloat in water. Life vest or life preserver.
life preserver (n) See life jacket.
life raft (n) Inflatable boat or floating flat structure used at sea in the event of an emergency. Found on an aircraft or a ship.
life vest (n) See life jacket.
life-belt (n) A large buoyant/floating ring used to keep a person afloat in water in an emergency.
lifeboat (n) **1.** Small boat carried by a ship which people can use to escape if there is any danger of the ship sinking or in the event of an emergency. **2.** Rescue boat sent out help people if they are in danger at sea.
lifeboat drill (n) An exercise or activity on a ship to familiarise the passengers with what they would have to do in an emergency, should they need to abandon ship.
lifeguard (n) A person who works at a swimming pool or a section of beach, who

rescues people when they are in danger of drowning.

lift (n) Mechanical platform which travels between floors within a building (UK). Elevator (US).

light aircraft (n) Small aeroplane that can only carry a few passengers.

lilo (n) Inflatable rubber or plastic bed that is used by holiday makers to float on the sea or lie on while sunbathing.

limousine (n) Large car with a driver.

liner (n) Large passenger ship, often used for cruises.

linkman (n) Doorman who stands outside a luxury hotel.

Lira (n) Italian unit of currency.

L.I.S. (abbr.) Liability Insurance Surcharge (car hire)

listed building (n) Building of historical merit protected legally, so that it cannot be demolished or altered without the permission of the local authority (UK).

liqueur (n) Strong alcohol based drink, usually consumed at the end of a meal.

llama (n) South American animal related to the camel but smaller and without humps. Recently introduced into Switzerland and used as a pack animal for cross-country treks.

load factor (n) Percentage occupancy of seats on transport.

L.O. (abbr.) Last Orders - e.g. for meals or drinks.

loading bay (n) Area where luggage or equipment is put onto transport.

lobby (n) Reception area in a hotel.

local authority (n) The people responsible for local government decisions, these people are usually members of borough councils, county councils, district councils and parish councils.

Local Area Initiative (n) Partnership between the public sector (tourist boards) and the private sector with clearly defined objectives.

local tax (n) The official tax in a region or a country.

local time (n) The official time in a region or a country.

locality (n) Immediate area in which someone lives or works.

location (n) Position where something or someone in situated or positioned.

locator (n) Computer booking reference, given by airlines and tour operators.

loch (n) Scottish or Irish lake, or inlet of the sea.

logistics (n) The planning of movement of equipment and/or people.

logo (n) Symbol or design, used by an organisation or a company as its sign.

long haul (n) Long distance flight, usually over 6 hours flying time.

long stay holiday (n) Holiday of more than three weeks.

longitude (n) Angular distance east or west on the earth's surface, measured in degrees from the prime meridian, 0°, which passes through Greenwich in London, England.

loss leader (adj.) Low price product or service, that does not make a profit, offered as an incentive to attract more customers to a company so that they will purchase profitable items in the future.

lost property (n) Personal possessions that have been lost, stolen or mislaid.

lost property office (n) Room where lost items are stored when they are found.

lough (n) See loch.

lounge (n) Seating area. Usually where people wait, such as in a hotel or departure lounge at an airport.

low season (adj.) The time of year when people do not usually go holiday, this usually coincides with the winter. Off season.

low tide (n) The time of the day when the sea level lowest. See tide.

luggage (n) Personal possessions packed in bags or cases for travelling. Baggage.
luggage room (n) Secure room set aside in hotels etc., for clients to leave luggage when checking out and having to wait for late departure.
lunch (n) Meal served in the middle of the day.

Mm - Mike

MA (abbr.) Via Mid-Atlantic.
macro economics (n) See external business environment.
mailing list (n) A list of names and addresses of people or organisations to which advertising or promotional material is sent.
mailshot (n) Advertising sent by post.
maitre d'hotel (n) Person in charge of the service in a restaurant.
management (n) The professional administration of business concerns.
manager (n) Person in charge, the most senior administrator.
manifest (n) List of passengers or cargo.
manual (n) Book of instructions and or company rules.
manual ticket issue (n) Issuing tickets for transport by hand, instead of by computer.
mansard (n) Windows that look like 'eyes' at top of 17th century French buildings.
map (n) A drawing or representation of an area of land, a city or a country, designed to represent locations in relation to each other, usually with a grid of lines across it, so particular locations can be found easily by noting where the lines of the grid intersect (grid reference).
M.A.P. (abbr.) Modified American Plan. Hotel accommodation including breakfast and one main meal.
maquis (n) Area of open uncultivated land found in southern France.
marina (n) Man-made harbour for boats and yachts, usually with long term berths for small boats.
Mark (n) German unit of currency.
mark-up (n) The difference between the cost of a product and the amount at which it is sold.
marker (n) Tall tour group member appointed by the tour guide, so the group can see this person in a crowd, this helps to keep the group together.
market (n) **1.** An area where traders set up stalls to sell goods. **2.** The amount of people who want, or who are able to buy a product.
market research (n) Study of needs or requirements of customers to find out how and why they buy goods or services.
market segmentation (n) A method of dividing potential customers into groups with distinctive characteristics, using criteria such as age, gender, area of residence, and income.
market share (n) Proportion of the total sales of a particular product or service gained by a particular company.
market value (n) The price that potential purchasers are prepared to pay for goods and services.
marketing (n) The planning and action of promoting and selling a product.
marketing communications (n) Process by which an organisation will promote a product to existing or potential customers - e.g. direct marketing, advertising.
marketing mix (n) the factors which a company can vary in trying to achieve its desired level of sales, including the product itself, its price, where it can be obtained and how it can be promoted.
marketing objectives (n) Aims of an organisation when undertaking a marketing campaign.
marketing personnel (n) Employees that

marketing personnel (n) Employees that are involved within the different areas involved with the marketing of a product.
marketing strategy (n) The entire marketing campaign that enables an organisation to reach the marketing objectives.
marquee (n) Large tent, usually hired for special occasions.
mass tourism (n) Movement of large numbers of people in relation to tourism - i.e. tourists and employees of tourism companies and attractions.
mast (n) Tall upright pole that supports the sails on a boat/yacht.
master key (n) Hotel key that can unlock all of the rooms in the hotel and is used by hotel staff to gain access to rooms for cleaning etc..
Mayday Mayday (adj.) International radio distress call.
matinee (n) Afternoon performance in a theatre or cinema.
M.B.O. (abbr.) Maintenance and Buildings Officer.
M.C.O. (abbr.) Miscellaneous Charges Order. Airline voucher used to cover collection of funds.
M.C.T. (abbr.) Minimum Connect Time.
meander **1.** (n) Large bend in a river. **2.** (v) When a road, river, trail etc. follows a course which has a lot of bends. **3.** (v) To walk somewhere in a leisurely or aimless way.
media (n) The method by which information is passed to the public, this is associated with newspapers, radio and television.
medical kit (n) Pack that contains the basics needed to deal with minor accidents. By law, in most countries, coaches, planes and other forms of public transport have to carry a medical kit.
Mediterranean (n) Sea between Europe and Africa. Also used to describe the areas of southern Europe that border the Mediterranean sea.
meet and greet (n) A service welcoming visitors as they arrive at a port of entry.
meeting (n) When a group of people come together for discussion.
megalith (n) A large stone that was sited by people, possibly as a monument, between 3000 - 2000 BC. - i.e. Stonehenge is a collection of megaliths arranged in a circle.
M.E.L. (abbr.) Minimum Equipment List (aircraft).
menu (n) List, usually of different types of food available.
merchandising (n) Products which are used to entice potential customers.
meridian (n) A line on a map passing through the North Pole and the South Pole.
metro (n) Underground system, particularly associated with Paris. See underground.
M.G.C. (abbr.) Museums and Galleries Commission.
M.I.A. (abbr.) Meetings Industry Association.
mic. (abbr.) Microphone.
Michelin (org.) French Tyre manufacturer that publishes maps and guide books. These products were originally designed to encourage travellers to drive cars, and, therefore, use Michelin tyres. Michelin developed a series of maps to make it easier for drivers to go from place to place. Also published are restaurant and hotel guides, and country/area guides, all to encourage car travel.
Michelin Star (n) Michelin guides grade the best restaurants and give them from one to three stars based on their general standard. Three stars being the maximum and representing the highest standard.
micro economics (n) See internal business environment.
microphone (n) Device which turns

microphone (n) Device which turns sound into electrical signals. Usually used to make sound louder (amplify it via speakers), or to record it (with audio recording equipment).

Middle East (n) Countries bordering Eastern Mediterranean and the Persian Gulf including Bahrain, Egypt, Iran, Iraq, Israel, Jordan, Kuwait, Lebanon, Oman, Palestine, Qatar, Saudi Arabia, United Arab Emirates and Yemen.

midnight sun (n) Found within the Arctic Circle when there are nights without darkness. This occurs in midsummer when the sun can often be seen shining at midnight. Many visitors make special trips to northern Scandinavia during mid-June to see this phenomenon.

midweek (n) Usually refers to Tuesday, Wednesday and Thursday - i.e. a midweek holiday does not include the weekend.

milk run (n) Tour that is easy to sell tickets for, because it follows the most popular, and generally overcrowded, routes.

minibar (n) Small refrigerator in hotel bedrooms or ship cabins, stocked with drinks, snacks etc..

minibreak (n) A short holiday away from home.

minimum stay (n) The shortest time before traveller can use the return section of a ticket, without paying a higher fare - i.e. A return ticket from London to Paris costs less if you stay in Paris for a minimum of three nights.

minutes (n) **1.** Division of time, 60 minutes = 1 hour. **2.** Formal written record of a meeting. 3. A division of degrees on a map, 1 degree (1˚) = 60 minutes (60').

mirage (n) Illusion created by hot air bending light rays, usually distortions that look like water, but, sometimes other objects can be reflected and become visible.

mishandled luggage (n) Luggage damaged while in transit with an airline.

misrouted luggage (n) Luggage that has been misplaced or sent to the wrong destination by an airline.

mission statement (n) A statement from the company that describes a company's present position and future objectives that is meant to create a united attitude among the employees.

mobile 1. (adj.) Portable or movable. **2.** (slang) mobile telephone.

moderator (n) Person who is in charge of discussions at a conference or meeting.

modular (n) **1.** Exhibition stands that are of standard sizes and are used at many different exhibitions. **2.** Courses that use the same lectures and material in units or modules. Each unit can be taught individually, without direct reference to other units.

mogul (n) Large hump on a ski slope.

money back (n) Return of sum of money paid for a particular product or service, especially if it is not satisfactory or faulty.

monsoon (n) **1.** Wind that blows across the Indian Ocean which blows from the north west in the winter and the south west in the summer. **2.** Wet weather season during the summer in regions of Southern Asia and the Far East that comes with the summer monsoon.

moor 1. (n) Open uncultivated land (UK). **2.** (v) To attach a boat or ship to land or a fixed point.

mosaic (n) Picture or design made by inlaying small pieces of coloured glass or stone in mortar.

motel (n) Hotel catering for car travellers, which provides parking space near to the rooms.

mothers' room (n) See parents' room.

motivator (n) Something that stimulates the interest of a potential tourist and effects his or her choice.

motorhome (n) A luxury caravan with integral drivers' compartment.

M.P.H. (abbr.) Miles Per Hour - a measurement of speed of a car, train, lorry etc..

M.P.P.A. (abbr.) Million Passengers Per Annum.

M.T.A.A. (abbr.) Multiple Travel Agents Association.

mule (n) **1.** Person used by a smuggler to carry illegal substances or goods on their behalf. **2.** A cross breed of a horse and a donkey.

multilateral (n) Involving three or more countries.

multiple use (n) The use and control of a resource for different purposes.

multiplex (n) A cinema in which a number of films can be screened simultaneously in different auditoriums.

multiplier effect (n) When the expenditure on one economic activity, such as tourism, has an effect on the turnover of other businesses in the same location.

multi-screen projection (n) Different images projected onto different screens at the same time.

multi-sector (adj.) Several sectors or portions - i.e. a company that works in more than one sector of the travel industry by providing hotel accommodation and travel.

museum (n) Building or venue housing items of historical, scientific and/or local importance.

Museums Association (org.) Independent organisation in the UK, founded in 1989 to improve and maintain standards, raise awareness of issues affecting museums and to represent the interests of museums at all levels of government.

M.V. (abbr.) Motor Vessel.

Nn - November

NA (abbr.) Via North-Atlantic.

N/A (abbr.) Not Applicable or Not Available.

N.A.H.C. (abbr.) National Association of Holiday Centres.

NAITA (acr.) National Association of Independent Travel Agents.

nanny (n) A person who is paid by parents to look after their child or children.

narrow boat (n) Boats used on canals, often hired out for holidays (UK).

National Breakdown (org.) Car rescue service.

national park (n) A large area of land which has been taken over and protected by Government or national authority because of its natural beauty. Probably the first National Park was Yellowstone, designated a National Park by US Congress in 1872. British National Parks were started in 1949 by the National Parks and Access to the Countryside Act.

National Trust (org.) Charitable organisation that preserves houses and countryside (UK).

nationality (n) To have been born in a particular country, therefore, have a legal right to be citizen and to be able to live in the country.

native **1.** (n) Belonging to a particular country - i.e. being born/brought up in a particular country. **2.** (adj.) To be of a particular country.

nautical mile (n) Measurement of distance by sea or air. 1 nautical mile = approx. 1.85 km or 1.15 miles.

N.E.A. (abbr.) National Exhibitors Association.

necessities bag (n) Given to airline passengers who have lost their luggage, it contains basic necessities such as washing kit etc..

neck mike (n) Microphone worn on a chain around the neck.

negative (adj.) No.

Neoplan (org.) German coach manufacturing company well known for making double-deck coaches.

net profit (n) The money that remains at the end of any given trading period after all the fixed costs have been paid.

network (n) **1.** A method by which computers are linked/connected together that enables information to be passed from computer to another. **2.** A group of interconnected organisations/individuals.

'new' tourist (n) Term used to describe travellers who are more environmentally aware, independent and demand greater flexibility in their travel and holiday arrangements.

next of kin (n) A person's closest living relatives or family.

niche marketing (n) Marketing directed to a particular section of the market that has its own special needs or interests - e.g. particular age groups.

night club (n) Place of entertainment open at night. Usually serves alcoholic drinks, sometimes food and has facilities for dancing.

night manager (n) Senior member of staff in charge of hotel at night.

night porter (n) Often only porter on duty at night, duties may include supervising the reception desk, the check-in of late arrivals, and supplying food if the hotel offers 24 hour room service.

night sheets (n) Covers used to protect an exhibition stand at night, while the exhibition is closed.

N.I.T.B. (abbr.) Northern Ireland Tourist Board.

NM (abbr.) Via North and Mid-Atlantic.

N.N.E.B. (abbr.) Nursery Nurse Examination Board. A qualification that is often needed to work supervising children for a tour operator.

non-revenue (n) A service or goods for which no charge can be made.

no show (adj.) Guest, delegate or passenger with a reservation who does not claim their reserved place.

N.O.E.A. (abbr.) National Outdoor Events Association.

nomad (n) Member of tribe that moves from area to area with no permanent living place.

noon (n) Midday, 12 o'clock in the day.

NP (abbr.) Via North or Central-Pacific.

Nordic (n) Of, or from Scandinavian countries (Northern Europe).

Northern Lights (n) Aurora Borealis.

North Pole (n) The most northern point of the world.

nose (n) Front end of an aircraft.

Nosub (abbr.) Not subject to load.

notice (n) Announcement, bulletin or sign giving instructions.

nozzle (n) Outlet or pipe delivering cooled air or liquid.

N.T. (abbr.) National Trust.

N.T.O. (abbr.) National Tourist Office/Organisation.

N.R.A. (abbr.) National Rivers Authority. UK Government Agency established in 1989 that is responsible for pollution control and protecting environment. The N.R.A. also promote leisure and recreation on rivers etc.. They also sample the quality water around the UK coast.

N.V.Q. (abbr.) National Vocational Qualification.

Oo - Oscar

O.A.G. (abbr.) Official Airlines Guide.

OAG Publications (org.) Reference publications for tourism industry.

O.& D. (abbr.) Origin and Destination.

oasis (n) Fertile place, which has a natural water supply, in a desert.

O.A.P. (abbr.) Old Age Pensioner.

objective (n) The desired or planned result.

observation area (n) An area at an airport where people can watch aircraft take off and land.

obstruct (v) To be in the way of or to block the passage of somebody or something.

ocean (n) The major seas that cover 70% of the world's surface.

oceanarium (n) Display of sea animals that is open to the public.

oceanography (n) Scientific study of the oceans.

occupancy (n) The amount of people using a facility or venue.

occupancy rate (n) Percentage of clients that have seats, hotel rooms, cruise cabins etc. at a particular time.

off duty (adj.) When someone is officially not working.

off-line (n) Countries/cities through which a carrier does not operate or have traffic rights to pick up passengers.

off loaded (v) When people or goods are taken from, or leave transport.

off peak (adj.) A period of time when demand is usually low.

off season (n) The time of year when people do not usually go on holiday - this usually coincides with the winter months.

officer (n) **1.** Official representative of a structured organisation. **2.** Senior crew member usually in charge of passengers and crew on a ship or an aircraft etc..

O.F.T. (abbr.) Office of Fair Trading.

O.H.P. (abbr.) Over Head Projector.

O.K. (adj.) When written on an airline ticket it means return flight does not have to be re-confirmed, or has already been re-confirmed.

on-board (adj.) To be situated in or on transport.

on foot (n) Walking.

on line (n) Connections by the same airline.

on site (adj.) On the premises.

one way (n) Single outward journey.

onshore (adj.) To be on land.

OPEC (acr.) Organisation of Petroleum Exporting Countries: Algeria, Gabon, Indonesia, Iran, Iraq, Kuwait, Libya, Nigeria, Qatar, Saudi Arabia, United Arab Emirates and Venezuela, which periodically fixes the price of oil. As a major portion of airline costs are for fuel, when this organisation increases prices it has a 'knock-on effect' on airline ticket and travel pricing.

open date (n) Return portion of ticket that can be used on any day and without an advance reservation.

open jaw (n) Airline ticket that allows stop-overs and/or different routes on the outward and inward journeys.

open space concept (adj.) At meetings and conferences delegates have no set agenda.

open skies (n) Air space not regulated by any government or organisation.

opening stock (n) Value of a company or organisation's stock at the beginning of a trading period.

operations room (n) Control room for coach operators, airlines, tour operators giving the latest travel information and co-ordinating events.

operator (n) Company offering tours and/or transport.

option (n) **1.** Choice or alternative. **2.** A holiday booking that has been reserved for a client and the option gives the client time to confirm the booking by paying for it or to pay a deposit for the booking.

option form (n) A record of a client's details used by a travel agent that lists a client's preferences - e.g. desired resort, departure date.

option reference (n) The reference number used by a travel agent to register an

optional (adj.) Left to choice whether to pay or do something.
Ordnance Survey (org.) Official map-making organisation in UK. It gets its name because the first maps were made for the army. Ordnance means artillery.
Ordnance Survey Maps (n) Very detailed large scale maps of all areas of the UK.
organic (adj.) Method of producing food crops that does not use artificial chemicals or fertilisers.
orientation tour (n) Short familiarisation tour on arrival in a town or city. Usually carried out by Courier or Tour Manager, not a local guide.
O.R.V. (abbr.) Oesterreichischer Reiseburo Verband. Austrian Travel Agent's Association.
O.S. (abbr.) Ordnance Survey.
out of pocket expenses (n) Personal money paid out on behalf of a company which will be reimbursed, by the company to the person, at a later stage.
out of service (n) **1.** When a room cannot be let for some reason - e.g. redecoration. **2.** (n) When something is not working. e.g. A lift or vending machine.
outbound (n) People or transport going out from, or leaving an area or country.
outskirts (n) Suburbs of a town or city.
outward (n) Departing leg of a return journey.
over (adj.) During radio communication 'over' signifies that information has been given and it is now the other communicators turn to talk/reply.
overbooking (n) Numbers booked exceed amount of places available.
overcharge (v) To unintentionally or intentionally charge someone too much money for goods or services.
overhead projector (n) Equipment which projects an image onto a screen from a large transparency.
overhead stowage lockers (n) Installed in coaches and aircraft to provide, closed containers for storing passengers hand luggage.
overlook (v) To forget or ignore something.
overnight bag (n) Bag carried as hand luggage containing basic necessities for overnight journey or one night away.
overriding commission (n) **1.** Extra commission paid to a travel agent who reaches a sales target. **2.** Additional money paid by a principal tour operator to an agent who is the middleman between the sales agent and the principal tour operator. The amount paid is based on the level of sales of the sales agent.
ozone (n) Form of oxygen found especially in the upper atmosphere of the Earth, which blocks some of the sun's harmful rays.

Pp - Papa

P (abbr.) Premium First Class air fare.
P.A. (abbr.) Public Address system.
P.A.I. (abbr.) Personal Accident Insurance.
package/package tour/package holiday (n) A holiday that is arranged by a tour operator and bought by customers, that includes accommodation, travel and food.
Package Travel Directive (n) European Union Directive, the full name of which is the Package Travel, Package Holidays and Package Tours Directive. This directive sets legal standards for tour operators that cover travel, accommodation and/or services, for holidays or trips booked in any E.U. country regardless of the destination.
packed lunch (n) Cold meal that is prepared in advance and can be carried.
pampas (n) Grasslands and open areas of Southern America.
Paradore (n) Spanish government owned

chain of hotels built in a local Spanish style and offering traditional Spanish food.

parasol (n) A large umbrella that protects people from the sun's rays.

parents' room (n) A room at an airport terminal where parents can attend to their children's needs such as feeding, nappy changing etc.. Parents' rooms can now also be found at railway stations and other transport terminals.

parish (n) **1.** An area in England that has it's own elected council. **2.** A village or an area of a town that has it's own church.

park (n) A public area with grass and trees that people can go to relax. Usually found in towns and cities.

park and ride (n) Where visitors are encouraged to park their cars outside an urban area (town or city) and ride into the centre of the town/city on a bus to prevent congestion from cars in the town or city.

Pars (n) C.R.S. for airlines including TWA and Northwest Airlines.

part charter (n) When only some of the seats on an aircraft are chartered by a tour operator(s).

partition (n) Movable interior wall.

partner (n) **1.** Accompanying person. **2.** Airline with which another has route sharing agreement.

passenger (n) A person travelling in or on transport.

passenger load (n) The total number of people travelling on a particular journey - i.e. train journey, flight, bus journey.

passive (adj) Term used when interpreting. The passive language you interpret from into the active language. e.g.From Croat - passive (language of delegate) into English - active (language from which most translators can translate into their own language.

passport (n) An official identity document that is used by people to enter countries other than one's own.

passport control (n) The place at an airport/border or port where visitors have to present their passports for official inspection, when entering/leaving a country.

P.A.T.A. (abbr.) Pacific Asia Travel Association.

PAX (acr.) Passengers.

paying-in slip (n) The document used to prove that money has been paid into a bank

payment received sheet (n) A record of all the incoming money.

payroll (n) The gross pay of all employees of a company, including all contributions by the employer and employee to National Insurance and other schemes.

P.C.O. (abbr.) Professional Conference Organiser.

P.C.V. (abbr.) Passenger Carrying Vehicle.

peak season (n) See high season

peak time (n) The time when demand for a product or service is at its' highest and, therefore the price is higher.

peninsula (n) A long piece of land that is almost completely surrounded by sea that is attached to other land at one point only.

pension (n) Small European hotel, often without a restaurant.

performance targets (n) Standards that are required by a company that enables the employees to measure how efficiently they are doing the job that they are requires to do by the employer.

perk/perks (n) A special benefit to someone doing a particular job - e.g. working for an airline means that the employees get cheap air fares.

permit **1.** (v) To allow. **2.** (n) Official pass or authorisation.

person specification (n) A description of the skills that are required by a potential employer from a potential employee.

personal space (n) The area around an

individual, which if a stranger enters the person is worried, frightened, embarrassed or annoyed. Everyone has their own definition of personal space, and some nationalities will permit closer contact than others.

personality girl/ model/ staff (n) Temporary staff used to add glamour to an exhibition or conference.

Peseta (n) Spanish unit of currency.

PEST analysis (n) The internal and external environmental factors within which an organisation operates - Potential, Economical, Social, Technological.

petty cash voucher (n) The document that is completed when money is spent on items of small value - e.g. coffee, stamps, stationary.

PEX (acr.) Public Excursion fare. Discounted fare offered by an airline or train company to passengers booking and travelling on the same day on specified routes.

P.G. (abbr.) Paying Guest - usually in a private house.

photogrammetry (n) Using photos to obtain measurements, particularly for making maps.

physical carrying capacity (n) The maximum amount of people that a facility has been designed to accept at any one time.

picnic (n) A meal eaten outdoors, usually sitting on the grass or on the beach.

pilgrim (n) Person who travels for religious reasons usually to visit a shrine, temple or other site of religious importance.

pilgrimage (n) A pilgrim's journey.

pilot 1. (n) Crew member who flies an aircraft and is responsible for the passengers and other crew. **2.** (n) Registered official who guides large ships into a harbour or guides large ships through dangerous waters. **3.** (v) To steer or guide a ship or an aircraft.

pipeline money (n) Money that has been paid to a travel agent by a client, but the money has not been passed to the principal.

P.I.R. (abbr.) Property Incident Report. Used for lost luggage.

pirate (n) Someone who is operating illegally.

piste (n) A track of firm snow for skiing on.

pit stop (n) A quick stop for refreshments when on a journey.

pitch 1. (n) Distance between the front edge of one seat and the seat behind. **2.** (v) To erect or put up a tent.

place of origin (n) The country, town, city where someone or something has originated from.

P.L.A. (abbr.) Port of London Authority. Governing body for the River Thames (UK).

place card (n) A small card that has a person's name written on it, which is put on a table at a formal meal to indicate where that person is to sit.

plastic (slang) Credit cards or charge cards.

plat du jour (n) Dish of the day. Chef's dish of the day in a restaurant or hotel (Fr.).

platform (n) **1.** The area of a railway station where passengers embark and disembark from the train. **2.** A raised stage or horizontal surface that is used by speakers or performers to enable them to be seen.

P.L.C. (abbr.) Public Limited Company (UK).

plenary session (n) Session in which all delegates participate.

plongeur (n) Person who is employed to wash up dishes etc. in a hotel or restaurant.

ploughman's lunch (n) Meal consisting of bread, cheese and pickle - often served in country pubs (UK).

P.M. (abbr.) Afternoon or evening.

pocket flight guide (n) Small timetables

carried by frequent flyers to help make last-minute flight arrangements

podium (n) Raised platform on which someone stands or sits.

polder (n) A Dutch (Netherlands) word for land that has been reclaimed from the sea. Usually farmland.

pollution (n) The introduction of an alien and usually damaging item into the environment. This can be refuse, industrial waste, fumes, noise or any other item that is considered undesirable in the location.

pool **1.** (n) Swimming pool. **2.** (v) Agreement where two or more transport carriers agree to promote one route and divide the revenue obtained from the route. **3.** (v) Agreement to collect tips or revenue and divide them up equally.

pooling (n) Two or more airlines may agree to pool the revenue to be obtained on a particular route.

population (n) The number of people that inhabit an area or country.

port (n) **1.** Harbour for ships. **2.** Also nautical/aviation term for the left side of a boat, ship or an aircraft when looking at it from the rear/back.

port charge (n) Charged by local authorities to passengers to pay for port facilities.

port-hole (n) The window in a ship or boat.

port tax (n) See Port Charge.

porter (n) Person who carries luggage at a hotel, hospital, railway station airport etc..

porterage (n) The act of carrying luggage.

portfolio of products (n) A list or range of products.

post- (prefix) After - e.g. Post-Conference tour = tour that takes place after a conference finishes.

postcard (n) A thin piece of card, usually with a picture on one side.

poster session (n) Display by the authors of scientific/technical and/or academic papers. Not generally a formal part of a conference, but ancillary.

pound (n) **1.** The unit of currency used in UK. Also used in other countries. See countries of the world. **2.** A unit of weight mainly used in UK and US.

pousada (n) Portuguese Government owned hotel built in local Portuguese style that offers Portuguese food.

powder skiing (n) Off-piste skiing on fresh snow.

powder snow (n) New snow that has just fallen.

P.R. (abbr.) Public Relations. Planned effort by an organisation to build a good relationship with the media (newspapers, television etc.) to gain publicity.

prairies (n) Large area of grassland found in North America. Prairies have very few trees.

pre- (prefix) Before - e.g. Pre-Conference tour = tour that takes place before a conference starts.

pre-arrival checks (n) Checks carried out before clients arrive, usually to confirm transport, accommodation, arrival time.

pre-assigned (adj.) Allocated beforehand.

pre-board passengers (n) Passengers allowed onto transport in advance of other passengers - i.e. disabled passengers boarding an aircraft first.

preferential (adj.) Giving an advantage - i.e. preferential rate.

preliminary draft (n) First version of a paper or document which is subject to further amendment.

premises (n) Buildings that are used by a business or organisation.

premium payment (n) A single payment that is paid for insurance.

premium traffic (n) Passengers paying higher fares - i.e. Passengers paying business or first class fares on airlines.

prepaid (adj.) Paid in advance.

preservation (n) The protection of an his-

historic building or an area of land.

press release (n) Leaflet/information sent to journalists and the media (newspapers/magazines/journals), that publicises a new product or service.

pressure group (n) A group or organisation who try and persuade people in authority (local/national governments) to take a specific course of action.

pressurised (adj.) When the air pressure in an aircraft cabin is kept as near to that of sea level as possible.

Prestel (org.) British Computerised Information System, generally used in Travel Agencies.

prevailing wind (n) The most frequent wind direction at a location.

primary data (n) The information obtained from the research that a company/organisation has commissioned.

primary research (n) See field research.

principal/s (n) The company or companies that a travel agency does business with - e.g. a coach company, an airline or a ferry company.

private facilities (n) En-suite bathroom.

private sector (n) Businesses that are owned by independent people and companies.

privatise (v) When a business that is converted from the public sector to the private sector.

pro rata (adj.) Agreement to divide up revenue.

P.R.O. (abbr.) Public Relations Officer. Person responsible for public relations.

product knowledge (n) The information that needs to be known in order to promote a product - e.g. the cost that the customers are prepared to pay.

product life cycle (n) The process which a product undergoes. This includes a product's conception, launch, establishment in the market place, and finally the product's decline.

product positioning (n) Selecting the correct target market and the distribution of a product that will maximise sales.

profit and loss account (n) A financial statement that describes a company's financial performance over a set period of time. This set period of time is usually one year.

profit margin (n) The percentage of the selling cost not accounted for by any of the production costs.

proforma (n) An invoice raised in advance of a booking, when a company or service provider requires payment in advance.

programme (n) Timetable of events.

projector (n) Machine that displays films and slides on a screen.

promotion (n) Event that increases the public's awareness of goods, services, venue etc..

promotional fare (n) Fares at a specially reduced price to encourage the use of a route or a method of transport.

promotional mix (n) See marketing mix.

promotional tool (n) The method by which a company/organisation will communicate with the potential customers in order to maximise sales - e.g. advertising, public relations.

property report (n) A report filled in by Reps. giving state of self catering accommodation.

proprietor (n) The owner of a hotel, guest house, shop, business etc..

P.R.S. (abbr.) Performing Rights Society. An organisation that issues licences that enables people to play music on coaches and in a public places.

P.S.A. **1.** (abbr.) Passenger Shipping Association. **2.** (abbr.) Passenger Service Agent - Airline receptionist.

P.S.V. (abbr.) Public Service Vehicle.

P/U (abbr.) Pick-Up - i.e. to pick up passengers.

pub (n) A building that has one or more bars that is licensed to sell alcoholic and non alcoholic drinks to the public. Public house (UK).
public holiday (n) Day during which all government offices and banks are closed.
public house (n) See pub.
public liability insurance (n) Insurance carried to ensure that passengers are covered in the event of an operator being accountable for a mishap or accident.
public sector (n) An organisation that is supported/financed by government funds/money.
public transport (n) Transportation owned by the state (government) such as buses and trains, that is used by the public buying their own tickets.
publicity (n) Information or actions that makes a person or place better known to the public.
pull **1.** (v) To attract. **2.** (n) An attraction. **3.** (v) To cancel. **4.** (slang) Removing voucher from an airline ticket when checking in.
pull factors (n) Positive features that attract tourists to a site or facility.
Pullman (n) A railway company or a railway carriage that offers extreme luxury to the passengers.
Pullman car (n) A railway carriage that provides beds for people to sleep in (US). See sleeping car (UK).
punctual (adj.) To be on time.
punctuality (n) The act of being on time.
Punt (n) Pound. Unit of currency in Eire (Republic of Ireland).
punter (slang) Passenger, client or customer.
purser (n) Person in charge of the welfare of the passengers on a ship or an aircraft.
Pusada (n) Portuguese Government owned hotel.
push factors (n) Negative features that motivate tourists to leave a site or facility.

Qq - Quebec

Q. & A. session (abbr.) Question and Answer session, usually at the end of a meeting, speech or discussion.
Q/C aircraft (abbr.) Quick Change aircraft. An aircraft that can easily convert between carrying passengers and/or freight.
quake. (abbr.) Earthquake.
qualification (n) Skill, experience, or examination passed, that makes a person suitable for a particular vacancy or job.
qualitative data (n) Data concerned with an organisation's position in a specific marketplace - i.e. visitors' opinions of one tourist attraction in comparison to another.
quality **1.** (n) The standard of goods or services when compared with similar goods or services. **2.** (adj.) Something which is of a high standard.
quality control (n) System for maintaining standards of goods and services.
QUANGO (acr.) Quasi-Autonomous Non-Governmental Organisation. A committee appointed by the government working independently. These committees have responsibility for particular areas of activity - i.e. the giving of government grants.
quantitative data (n) Factual data concerned with an organisation - i.e. the exact number people that visited a tourist attraction during a specific period of time.
quarantine (n) Period of time during which humans or animals are kept away from others to reduce the risk of disease spreading, because they may be or are infected.
quay (n) Platform next to the sea or a river where boats or ships can berth, load and unload.
queen size bed (n) Double bed.
questionnaire (n) A form used to gather information, by asking questions.
queue (n) People or vehicles in line one

information, by asking questions.

queue (n) People or vehicles in line one behind the other that are waiting for something.

quicksand (n) Wet sand which can be dangerous, as normally it will not support the weight of a person.

quilt (n) Duvet.

quota (n) Quantity or size of official allocation.

quote (n) Price or estimate for goods or services.

Rr - Romeo

R (abbr.) Concorde Class.

RAC (org.) A vehicle rescue service (UK).

rack (n) Ledges or shelves above or at the ends of seats on transport, where passengers can store their luggage.

rack rate (n) Normal price for a hotel room to individual clients.

racking (v) The displaying of travel brochures in a travel agency.

reconciliation (n) The receipts and payments of a company after a set period of time - e.g. weekly or monthly.

radar (n) A system of locating the position and speed of objects such as aircraft and ships when they cannot be seen. This is done by the use of radio signals.

rails (n) Metal bars on which train wheels run.

railway (n) Company that provides transport by train.

Ramadan (n) Islamic religious event which takes place in the ninth month of the Muslim calendar. During Ramadan Muslims do not eat between sunrise and sunset.

ramp (n) **1.** Sloping passage to make wheelchair access easier. **2.** Steps leading up to an aircraft.

Rapide (n) Brand name for National Express Coaches which have host/hostess refreshment service.

rapids (n) Section of a river which is fast flowing, often shallow and rocky.

rapporteur (n) Official who is appointed to attend a conference or meeting and write a report or a summary.

rate of exchange (n) The price at which one currency is valued compared with other currencies.

R.C.I. (abbr.) Resort Condominiums International. Organisation that acts as a clearing house for time-share properties, worldwide, when the owners want to change or swap their holiday periods.

rebate (n) Refund of money after goods or services have been purchased.

re-book (v) To book or order again.

receipt (n) Formal written confirmation that goods or payment have been received.

reception (n) Area in a hotel, campsite, accommodation or other venue, where guests are welcomed, checked in, issued keys etc..

receptionist (n) Person who works in a reception area.

reclaimed land (n) Land that has been made usable for building or agriculture by draining or making a barrier against the sea, etc..

reclining seats (n) Seats that have an adjustable back which can be tilted backward or forward.

reconfirm (n) To confirm or check a booking that has already been made.

reconfirmation (v) Passengers who break their journey at any point for more than seventy-two hours may be required to reconfirm their intention to use their next reservation.

recreation (n) Activity done for pleasure in time away from work.

recycle (n) To re-use resources - i.e. to re-use empty bottles.

reference (n) A statement by a person on behalf of a potential candidate that details the candidates suitability for a potential job/position. This is usually in written form but can also be done verbally.

refund (v) To pay money back after it has been spent. Rebate.

refreshments (n) Food and drink.

regatta (n) Event at which races are held between boats.

regeneration (n) The rebuilding of an area that is 'run down' because of lack of financial investment.

region (n) Area of land that is different from other areas of land because it has individual features.

register **1.** (n) Official record of attendance or people staying in a hotel. **2.** (v) To sign the official register of attendance or to check in at hotel or conference. **3.** (n) Log book of a ship.

registered baggage (n) Luggage given to the carrier and not the responsibility of the passenger until claimed at end of the journey.

registration (n) Check in for conference or exhibition.

registration form (n) Form on which delegates confirm booking for a conference, giving details of their requirements.

reimburse (v) To pay money back after it has been spent. Refund, rebate.

relay interpreter (n) An interpreter at a meeting who translates a minority language into a common language for the other interpreters to listen to and translate into their own language - e.g. a conference where a Romanian speaker is translated by relay interpreter into English and then other interpreters translate into Japanese, Arabic and German etc..

release date (n) The date at which an airline or hotel can sell seats or rooms to customers because the tour operator has not taken it's full allocation of seats or rooms.

remortgage (v) The borrowing of an additional sum of money against a property.

remote control (n) A handheld device for controlling electrical appliances, TV, video, etc.

rental charges (n) Money paid for the use or hire of equipment, vehicle or a venue.

Rep. (abbr.) Representative.

repatriation (n) To be brought home to a home country - e.g. Emergency repatriation insurance is taken out by travellers to ensure that when they are away from home, if they are seriously ill or injured, they can be flown home.

report (n) Official written details of events or happenings.

representative (n) Person appointed by a company to work at a resort or tourist area serving the needs of clients.

request (v) To ask politely for something.

research (n) Investigation or study to discover or establish facts.

reservation system (n) Procedure set up to enable an organisation to keep a record of what packages or services it has available for sale. C.R.S. is a computerised reservation system.

residence (n) Place where someone lives.

resort (n) Area with accommodation and facilities, especially for tourists.

resort representative (n) Person who represents a company in a resort or tourist area looking after the clients of that particular company.

resources (n) Things that an organisation has at its disposal that enables it to carry out trading - i.e. time, money, workforce.

responsible tourism (n) Sometimes called 'green' tourism. Tourism organised to help the local economy without being intrusive or damaging to the local environment.

rest room (n) Lavatory or toilet in a public

place (US).

retail audit (n) A survey measuring the volume of sales and the price of goods and services in a number of retail outlets.

retail travel (n) the selling of travel arrangements directly to customers.

restaurant (n) Public place where meals can be bought and eaten.

restaurant car (n) Carriage of a train where meals can be bought and eaten.

return (n) **1.** Leg of a journey that is coming back to the original point of departure. **2.** Ticket that includes the outward and inward legs of a journey.

revalidate (v) **1.** Officially reconfirm or reinstate. **2.** Officially change ticket and to make it valid for travel.

revalidation sticker (n) An attachment to flight coupon of an airline ticket when a change made to original reservation.

reveal (n) When a new product is shown to a sales force for the first time at a conference.

reverse thrust (n) Push or thrust of a jet engine when it is reversed, to act as a brake and to slow down an aircraft when landing.

ridge and furrow (n) Features in a field where ploughing, since the Middle Ages, has formed a set of parallel ridges.

rights of access (n) Terms and conditions specified by the property or site owner.

rip-off (slang) **1.** To intentionally charge someone too much money for goods and services. **2.** When something has cost too much money.

Riviera (n) Coastal area of natural beauty and good climate.

Rm (abbr.) Room.

road toll (n) The charge or fee for using a toll road.

R.O. (abbr.) Room only.

room service (n) Service in a hotel which provides snacks, meals and drinks and delivers them to a room.

rooming list (n) List showing the names of clients who have booked accommodation, and simple details of any extras that they may require.

ro-ro (abbr.) Roll on, roll off. Car ferry that allows cars to drive on and off. Normally loaded through the stern of the vessel and unloaded from the bows of the vessel.

roster (n) List of staff and the duties they have to perform at particular times.

rostrum (n) Raised platform on which a speaker stands or sits.

rotation (n) **1.** Round trip, made by an aircraft from base to destination and return to base. **2.** Moving passengers around in a coach to ensure each one has an opportunity to sit in the best seats.

round the clock (n) In operation or open 24 hours a day.

round trip (n) Outward and return journey.

route (n) **1.** Method or direction of travelling between two places. **2.** Regularly travelled course or path or direction between two places - i.e. bus or coach route. 3. Road (US).

roving mike (n) Microphone that is carried around.

R.P.K. (abbr.) Revenue Passenger Kilometres.

R/Q (abbr.) Request.

R.Q. (abbr.) Found on an airline ticket meaning the holder is requested to reconfirm flight.

R.S.A. (abbr.) Royal Society of Arts. Examination body (UK).

R/T (abbr.) Return Trip.

R.T. (abbr.) Round Trip.

R.T.F. (abbr.) Radiotelephone or Radiotelephony.

R.T.W. (abbr.) Round The World.

rucksack (n) A bag with straps that enables it to be worn over the shoulders. It is used by walkers or by climbers. Also

known as a pack or backpack (US).
rudder (n) **1.** A broad, flat movable piece of wood or metal at the stern (back) of a ship used for steering. **2.** Vertical moving surface, attached to the upright fin at the rear of an aircraft (tail), to control the horizontal movement of an aircraft.
runway (n) Landing and takeoff surface for aircraft.
rural tourism (n) Tourism based away from cities in the countryside.
R.Y.A. (abbr.) Royal Yachting Association.

Ss - Sierra

S.A. (abbr.) When written on an airline ticket it means the holder must reconfirm the flight booking.
Sabre (n) C.R.S. for American Airlines.
S.A.G.T.A. (abbr.) School And Group Travel Association.
safari (n) A tour or expedition to see or hunt wildlife especially in Eastern and Southern Africa.
safety announcement/ briefing (n) Verbal instructions on safety procedures usually given by a crew member of a ship or aircraft.
safety audit (n) Examination of the physical and operational aspects of a facility in order to identify the hazards and to minimise risks.
safety deposit box (n) Small lock-up safe provided in hotels, etc. for guests to secure their valuables/money etc..
safety drill (n) When passengers, visitors or guests are told what they have to do in the event of an emergency.
sail 1. (n) Large piece of material attached to the mast of a ship/yacht. When the wind blows against the sail, the ship/yacht will be moved forward. **2.** (v) To move a boat/yacht on water. **3.** (v) The actual movement of a vessel on water.
sales (n) See sales department.
sales department (n) Department within an organisation that is responsible for selling products/services.
salt flat (n) Dried up bed of a salt lake.
salt pan (n) Shallow dip or depression where salty water collects and then is dried out by the sun. The salt that is left is after the water has gone then collected for use elsewhere.
sampling (v) Method of collecting information from a sample group of people that enables companies and organisations to make predictions about the behaviour of the population in general.
S.A.R. (abbr.) Search and Rescue (Air).
saturated market (n) A market that cannot absorb any more of a specific product or service.
scenic (adj.) Having attractive natural landscape.
schedule (n) Timetable.
scheduled service (n) Regular transport service available to anyone paying a fare.
Schilling (n) Austrian unit of currency.
schuss (v) To ski downhill.
seamen's fares (n) Reduced air fares when ship's crew are travelling.
seasonal (adj.) When certain things happen at certain times of the year.
seasonality (n) The different requirements of tourists at different times of the year.
seat allocation (n) A specific seat for a specific person - e.g. seats on an aeroplane.
seat belt (n) Strong, well-anchored adjustable strap used to secure passengers in their seats while in transport.
seat only (n) Sale of seats only on an aircraft with no accommodation or other services included.
seat pitch (n) Distance between aircraft seats.
seating plan (n) A diagram showing the

restaurant, etc..

secondary spend (n) Money spent by visitors on items other than the entry fee. i.e. purchasing food and souvenirs.

sector (n) Defined part of a region, industry or market.

security (n) Procedures to ensure protection and safety of travellers etc..

security screening (n) Machines and trained personnel used to check luggage and passengers before they board transport to ensure that no explosive devices, weapons or other illegal goods are carried on board.

segment (n) Portion or section - usually of a journey.

self employed (adj.) Working independently, directly for clients or customers and not for an employer.

self-catering (adj.) Accommodation which provides guests with their own cooking facilities.

self-guided route/trail (n) When visitors are given a map, or follow signs on their own, without a guide.

seminar (n) When a group meets for discussion or training.

senior citizen (n) Elderly person or old age pensioner (O.A.P.).

service (n) Enterprise on a commercial basis that supplies peoples needs others - e.g. door to door home food delivery.

service charge (n) Amount of money added to a bill to cover the cost of waiting staff, usually in a restaurant.

service flats/ apartments (n) Accommodation that is half way between a hotel and self-catering.

service industry (n) An industry that supplies services and not goods.

serviced accommodation (n) See serviced flats/apartments.

set 1. (v) To lay out cutlery, plates etc.. **2.** (n) An arrangement on a platform, stage, etc..

set designer (n) A person who prepares the arrangements for a stage or conference platform.

set down (n) Place for passengers to alight from transport.

set meal (n) Meal with no choices of food provided.

set-up time (n) Period of time during which an exhibition or conference prepares to open; when stands, lighting, staging, etc. are arranged.

SGITS (acr.) Special Group Inclusive Tour rates.

shell (n) Cover or folder made of paper or stiff board, used to hold leaflets or as front cover of brochure.

shell folder (n) See Shell.

shell scheme (n) Basic stand at an exhibition.

shire (n) Anglo-Saxon English term for administrative district. The person in charge used to be called the Reeve - hence Shire-reeve which later became sheriff.

shoplifting (n) Illegal act taking goods from a shop without paying for them.

shore (n) The land along the edge of the sea or any large area of water.

shore excursion (n) Visit from a cruise ship to land.

shoreline (n) The edge of the sea or any large area of water.

short breaks (n) Holidays that last for a few days only.

short fall (n) The Amount that actual business is less than expected business.

short haul destinations (n) Destinations that are close to your country of departure - e.g. a short haul destination from the UK would be France, Belgium, Germany.

shoulder (n) Area or lane at the side of a motorway/highway restricted for emergency use.

shoulder period (n) Period between high and low season.
shuttle (n) Short, frequent, scheduled trips operated by aircraft or coaches; usually no advance reservation is needed.
sick bag (n) Heavy paper bag carried on transport for passengers to be sick (vomit) into if they are ill.
siesta (n) Traditional custom, particularly in Spain, where the shops are closed during the hottest part of day.
sightseeing (n) Tour round a tourist venue or area of interest.
silver service (n) Food service where waiters serve food to each guest at a table using a 'silver' serving spoon and fork.
simultaneous interpreting (n) Translating one language into another while the speaker is speaking.
single (n) **1.** Room for one person with one bed. **2.** Ticket for one person only. **3.** Ticket for a one way or outward journey.
single supplement (n) Extra fee paid by individual travellers in accommodation who require their own room.
single travel-to-work area (n) Term used by the Department of Employment to describe a commuting area.
Sirocco (n) Hot dry wind which blows across from Sahara over the South of France
site (n) Area such as park, ruin, Roman settlement etc..
S.I.T.E. (acr.) Society of Incentive Travel Executives.
site guide (n) Walking tour guide working in park, house or small area.
site inspection (n) Visit to look at facilities, location or venue.
six pm release (n) Around the world hotels will not hold a room after 1800 (6pm) local time if guest has not arrived by this time, unless a special arrangement is made.
ski evolutif (n) Ski training method using very short skis, replacing them with longer skis as the learner progresses or improves.
skipper (slang) Captain - usually of a ship, boat or ferry.
skyjack (n) When an airline is hijacked during flight.
slalom (n) Downhill ski race using poles to mark out the course.
sleep out (v) When a hotel guest does not use the room they booked and paid for.
sleeper (n) **1.** A train with beds for people to use in order to sleep on overnight journeys. **2.** A carriage of a train with beds for people to use in order to sleep on overnight journeys.
slide (n) Photographic transparency which can be used in a projector.
slide projector (n) Machine that shines a bright light through a photographic transparency (slide), magnifies this image and projects it onto a screen.
slot (n) The time allocated to an aircraft during which it can take off.
SMART (acr.) Suitable, Measurable, Attainable, Realistic, Targeted - the planned activities or objectives.
smart card (n) Plastic card, the same size as a credit card with built-in microchip memory that can have many functions.
smart card travel (n) New system where ticket details will be issued and stored electronically on a smart card. The card can then be passed through a machine at the airport instead of waiting at check-in.
smoke hood (n) A hood that is put over a person's head to provide protection against smoke inhalation in the event of a fire.
smuggle (v) To bring, take or send goods into a country secretly and illegally.
smuggler (n) Person who secretly and illegally brings goods into a country.

Usually to avoid paying duty or tax or because the goods are illegal.

S.N.A.V. (abbr.) Syndicat National des Agents de Voyages. French Association of Travel Agents.

S.N.C.F. (abbr.) Societé National de Chemins de Fer. French railways organisation.

sniffer dog (n) Dog that is trained to find drugs or explosives etc. by using its sense of smell.

snow cannon (n) Machine that makes and distributes artificial snow.

snow line (n) Level or height on a mountain above which snow is permanent.

social programme (n) Organised social events to entertain people on holiday or people attending a conference.

social tourism (n) Development and encouragement of services for disabled visitors and disadvantaged members of society.

solar (adj.) From the sun. Solar panels (solar energy) are used in many hotels in Mediterranean countries to generate power to heat water etc..

sommelier (n) Highly trained wine waiter (Fr).

son et lumiere (n) Sound and Light show at night (Fr).

sous chef (n) Assistant to the head chef.

sous vide (n) Food cooked in a central kitchen, away from the serving area, and then reheated before serving.

souvenir (n) Goods bought as gifts etc. that are typical or relate to the area where they are bought.

SP (abbr.) Via South Pacific.

spa (n) Place with a natural water spring.

S.P.A.A. (abbr.) Scottish Passenger Agents Association.

speaker (n) **1.** Someone who delivers a talk or speech at a meeting, conference or formal dinner. **2.** Part of a sound system from which sound comes.

Special Group Inclusive Tour rates (n) Scheduled airline seats that are specially priced for ITX.

special interest (n) Holidays catering for people interested in certain subjects or offering specialist lectures

special needs (n) Special requirements for passengers - e.g. disabled passengers have special needs.

speeding (n) When a vehicle is going faster than the speed allowed by law.

split charter (n) When two or more tour companies share the hire of an aircraft.

split shift (n) When staff start work in the morning, go off duty in middle of day, and return to work in the evening - split shifts are often worked in hotels and restaurants.

sponsor (n) Individual or a company giving support, usually financial, to an event.

spot rate (n) Exchange rate that is obtained by making an immediate transfer of currencies.

spotlight (n) Adjustable lights with a beam that can be focused into a small area or spot.

spouse (n) Husband or wife.

spouse events (n) Activities not directly related to a conference normally for entertainment that are part of the spouse programme.

spouse programme (n) Social programme to entertain people that accompany delegates to a conference while the conference is in session.

S.P.Q.R. (abbr.) Senatus Populas Que Romanus - for the Roman Senate and the People.

sprinter train (n) Local train service, usually with few carriages, that runs through the countryside connecting major towns and cities.

S.S.S.I. (abbr.) Site of Special Scientific Interest (on a map).

S.S.V. (abbr.) Supplementary Services Voucher.

S & T (abbr.) Shower and toilet.

stabiliser (n) Term for exclusive dealing arrangements - i.e. ABTA tour operators may only sell through ABTA retailers who can not sell non-ABTA tour operators' services. Normally this would be illegal, but it has been proved to offer protection for clients' money so it is allowed to continue.

stabilisers (n) Fins below the waterline on the sides of a ship, to stop the ship from rolling in the sea and make a voyage more comfortable for the passengers on board.

stalactite (n) Limestone column hanging from the roof of a cave, formed from calcium carbonate in water as it drips down from the cave roof.

stalagmite (n) Limestone column formed on the floor of a cave from the calcium carbonate in water. The column points up toward the cave roof.

stall (n) **1.** Table or small shop from which things are sold - i.e. market stall. **2.** Dangerous loss of speed of an aircraft at which it no longer has enough lift to fly, causing it to fall rapidly.

stalls (n) Seats in a theatre that are nearest the stage.

standby fare (n) Fare that does not guarantee a seat. Passengers with standby tickets can only travel if there are seats available through cancellation or all normal fare paying passengers have been seated and there are still available seats.

standby passenger (n) Passengers with no guaranteed seat on transport who wait for a seat to become vacant - e.g. in the event of a booking cancellation a seat will become available.

starboard (n) The right side of a ship or an aircraft when looking from the back towards the front.

starter (n) The first course that is served at a formal meal.

stately home (n) Large house or mansion, usually of historical interest.

statement of account (n) Document that is sent to a customer that shows all the business transactions with the supplier, whether the business transactions have been paid for or not.

stateroom (n) Large and comfortable room or cabin on a ship. Usually the best and most expensive accommodation on a ship.

station manager (n) **1.** Person in charge of a Railway station. **2.** Senior staff member of an airline responsible for ground handling at an airport.

status box (n) Section on an airline ticket showing if the ticket is for a confirmed or unconfirmed booking.

stay over (v) When a hotel guest is staying another night.

S.T.B. (abbr.) Scottish Tourist Board.

sterile (n) Term for an area that has been cordoned off and searched for security reasons. It remains sterile whilst under guard, but if people are let in without being searched, the area loses this status.

stern (n) Back end or rear of a ship.

steward (n) Male member of the crew of a ship or an aircraft who looks after the needs of passengers and serves food etc..

stewardess (n) Female member of the crew of a ship or an aircraft who looks after the needs of passengers and serves food etc..

stick time (n) Industry term for the time a pilot spends actually flying a plane.

S.T.O.L. (abbr.) Short Take Off and Landing (aircraft).

stone age (n) Period from about 250,000 BC to 2000 BC. First major phase of prehistoric culture, during this time tools and weapons were made from stone.

stop-over (n) Break in a long journey,

usually overnight - i.e. when flying from London to Australia many people stop-over in Bangkok or Singapore.

stow (v) To put away - e.g. luggage.

stowage lockers (n) Closed container shelves used for storing passengers' hand luggage.

stowaway (n) Person who travels illegally by hiding on transport.

strait (n) Narrow stretch of water linking two larger areas of water.

strategic alliance (n) Two or more companies/organisations that work together for mutual benefits or self interest.

strategic marketing (n) The process by which a strategic alliance achieves its aims - see strategic alliance.

strike (v) When workers refuse to work as a protest.

strip cultivation (n) In Europe and UK this was a mediaeval form of farming, where fields were divided into parallel strips.

study tour (n) Tour arranged for company or group interested in studying a special area or subject.

subcontractor (n) Company or person hired by the principal contractor to help with work.

subsidiary (n) a branch of a company/organisation that affects the overall financial results of the company as a whole.

subsonic (n) Below the speed of sound - i.e. subsonic aircraft fly slower than the speed of sound (1225 k.p.h. - 761 m.p.h.).

sustained yield (n) Use of resources in order to maintain their quality and quantity over a period of time which enables the same amount of customer satisfaction to be continued.

substitute (v) To replace someone who is unable to take up a seat or ticket, etc..

subway (n) **1.** U.S. underground or metro system. See underground. **2.** A path or passage that allows people to walk under a busy road or under a railway track (UK).

suite (n) Hotel accommodation with a bedroom, bathroom and separate sitting/living room.

summit (n) **1.** The highest point; Top. **2.** A meeting of high powered people.

sun cream/lotion (n) Cream or lotion that gives the skin some protection from the sun and helps to prevent sunburn.

sunbathe (v) To sit or lie outside where the sun shines in order to get a suntan.

sunburn (n) When the skin suffers burning or inflammation from exposure to sun's rays, often causing pain. Sunburn can also be caused by the sun's rays reflecting off water or snow even if the person has not been in direct sunlight.

sunglasses (n) Spectacles with dark lenses that protect the eyes from the sun's rays.

sunstroke (n) An illness that is caused by over exposure to heat from the sun.

supersonic (n) Faster than the speed of sound - i.e. supersonic aircraft fly faster than the speed of sound (1225 k.p.h. - 761 m.p.h.).

supplement (n) **1.** Additional charge for goods or services. **2.** Additional part of a timetable or book.

supplier (n) Company that provides services or goods.

surcharge (n) Extra or additional charge.

surface (n) Travelling on or by land.

sustainable tourism (n) Tourism that does not interfere with or damage the physical, social and cultural environment of an area.

Sustrans (org.) Charity which builds and designs routes for cyclists, wheelchair users and walkers.

S.V. (abbr.) Sea View.

SVQ (abbr.) Scottish Vocational

Qualifications.

S.W.B. (abbr.) Single With Bathroom. Single bedroom with en suite bathroom.

SWOT analysis (n) The overall assessment of a company's position by analysing the company's Strengths, Weaknesses, Opportunities and Threats.

syndicate (n) **1.** An association of individuals or commercial firms working together. **2.** Meeting for an association or group.

Tt - Tango

T (abbr.) When written on airline ticket denotes tourist or economy class.

tab (slang) Bill/account.

table d'hôte menu (n) Literally Host's table menu - menu in restaurant or cafe usually with one or few choices and a fixed price.

table plan (n) Diagram showing the location of tables at a function. It usually also shows, in alphabetical order, the names of guests and the tables at which they are sitting.

tacho. (abbr.) Tachograph.

tachograph (n) Device for recording distance travelled and the speed of a coach, bus or truck, and also the number of stops the driver makes.

tactical marketing (n) Marketing that is undertaken by an organisation when something unforeseen happens in the marketplace.

tail wind (n) Wind blowing from behind an aircraft, or other vehicle, making it travel faster.

tailor made (adj.) Holiday designed specially for a specific client.

take off (v) When an aircraft leaves the ground and begins to fly.

Tannoy (n) System of loud speakers used to make public announcements. Public address system (UK).

target markets (n) The potential consumer groups to which a business/organisation is aiming to sell their products and services.

tariff (n) **1.** List of charges. **2.** Tax or duty charged by a government on goods being brought into a country.

taverna (n) Inn (Greece).

taxi **1.** (n) Car, usually licensed by the local authorities, which can be hired by passengers to take them to a destination. **2.** (v) When aircraft moves to/from runway.

taxi meter (n) Device in a taxi or cab which measures the cost of a journey.

taxi way (n) Paved area for aircraft movement between the apron and the runway.

T.B.A. (abbr.) To Be Advised.

T.D.A. (abbr.) Timeshare Developers' Association.

T.D.D. (abbr.) Telecommunication Devices for the Deaf.

T.D.H. (abbr.) Table D'Hôte menu.

technician (n) Expert who has a particular skill or technique, usually mechanical.

T.E.E. (abbr.) Trans Europe Express railway trains.

teleconferencing (n) See audio conferencing.

temp. (abbr.) **1.** Temporary. **2.** Temporary worker.

temporary (n) **1.** Structure that is put up for a short time and will then be dismantled. **2.** A member of staff who fills a position for a short period of time and then leaves.

tenant (n) **1.** Self-employed person who runs a pub or bar that is owned by a brewery. **2.** Person who rents and lives in long term accommodation.

tender (n) **1.** Small boat that carries passengers between a larger boat and shore. **2.** Formal offer to supply goods or services and a statement of the price that will be charged.

tent (n) Portable shelter, usually made of

canvas, that is relatively easy to carry and to erect, to provide overnight accommodation.

terminal (n) Building for arrivals and departures - i.e. at an airport or bus depot.

terrace (n) **1.** A row of houses adjoining one another by their side walls (UK). **2.** A flat area of grass or stone next to a building where people can sit.

tertiary industry (n) Industry that provides goods and services for other industries.

T.E.S.A. (abbr.) The Events Suppliers Association.

T.G.V. (abbr.) Train a Grande Vitesse. French high speed train.

thermal spring (n) Naturally occurring hot water coming out from the ground.

theme park (n) Outdoor venue which is open to the public, that charges an entrance fee and has a theme or special interest.

themed break/holiday (n) Special interest break or holiday.

thin route (n) Airline route where demand for seats is low.

third age (n) Polite term for Old Age Pensioners.

three letter codes (n) The abbreviated identification codes used by cities and airports worldwide.

throughput capacity (n) Maximum amount of users that a facility can accommodate during a set period of time.

thrust (n) Force from a jet engine or propeller that makes aircraft go forwards.

T.I.A. (abbr.) Travel Industry Association of America.

T.I.C. (abbr.) Tourist Information Centre.

ticket (n) Official piece of paper or card to show that a person can travel on transport, enter a venue or has paid for something in advance.

ticket tout (n) Someone who offers tickets for entry to a popular event at a price higher than the official purchase cost. In the US these are known as Scalpers.

tide (n) Regular rise and fall of the sea level, caused by the attraction of the moon and sun. This happens twice every 24 hours.

till record (n) When a cash till or cash register prints a receipt, it also prints a copy of the receipt/transaction onto an internal till roll for the records of the company.

time series charter (n) Where a tour operator contracts an airline for the use of an aircraft for a specific length of time.

time zone (n) Area of the world where the time is calculated as being a particular number of hours ahead or behind G.M.T.. These areas are usually across 15° of longitude.

timeshare (n) Holiday accommodation that is owned by several people who can use it at different times of the year.

timetable (n) Schedule of events or travel times.

T.I.M.G. (abbr.) Tourist Industry Marketing Group.

tip (n) Gratuity given for good service.

toastmaster (n) Person at formal functions that announces the names of guests as they arrive, and has other ceremonial duties including the calling for silence so that guests can make speeches and propose toasts. In the UK they often wear a uniform with a red tailcoat and white bow tie.

T.O.C. (abbr.) Tour Operators' Council of ABTA.

TOD (acr.) Ticket on departure.

toilet (n) Lavatory or W.C..

toll (n) Charge or fee for using a toll road or a toll bridge.

tonnage (n) Weight measurement for the carrying capacity of a ship.

T.O.P. (abbr.) Tour Operators' Package fares.

TOPS (acr.) Thomson Holiday CRS system.

tornado (n) Violent wind storm at the centre of which is a funnel shaped cloud.

T.O.S.G. (abbr.) Tour Operators' Study Group.

tour conductor (n) Tour manager in charge of a group.

tour director (n) Person in charge of group of tourists. Level 4 N.V.Q. advanced qualification.

tour guide (n) Person in charge of coach group. Level 2 N.V.Q. basic qualification.

tour manager (n) Person in charge of coach group. Level 3 N.V.Q. intermediate qualification.

tour operator (n) Company that organises and manages package tours.

tourism (n) Temporary movement of people to destinations outside the places where they normally live and work, and their activities during their stay at these destinations.

tourism balance (n) Difference between the earnings that a country receives from inbound tourism and it's residents expenditure on overseas tourism - see inbound and outbound.

tourism services (n) Services offered by regional and national tourist boards, tourist attractions, accommodation etc..

tourist (n) Someone who spends a night away from home on holiday or business. Person who visits another area or country generally for a holiday or pleasure, but certain tourist statistics will include visits for business and medical treatment.

tourist board (n) Official office for promotion of a city, region or country.

tourist class (n) Least expensive class for air travel.

tourist enclave (n) Where tourist accommodation is separated from the local population, often for the security of the tourists.

townhouse hotel (n) Type of hotel offering luxury accommodation in renovated domestic buildings.

T.Q.M. (abbr.) Total Quality Management.

trade fair/show (n) Exhibition confined to people working in a specific industry or association that is not open to the general public.

Trade Descriptions Act 1968 (n) Legislated act making it illegal to make false or misleading claims about a product or service that could deceive purchasers (UK).

trading/profit and loss account (n) The record of sales and expenses during a trading period. When the costs have been deducted, the account will show either a net profit or a net loss.

traffic manager (n) Person in a coach company responsible for the day-to-day running and allocation of coaches.

trail (n) **1.** Designated route through the countryside. **2.** Walking tour, with a theme, in a town or city.

Tramontana (n) Cold dry wind blowing south starting from northern Italy and central Spain.

transcribe (v) To take write out in full a speech, talk, etc..

transcript (n) A written record of a speech, talk, etc..

transfer 1. (v) Move passengers from one location to another. **2.** (n) Ticket that allows passengers to continue their journey on another train or bus (US).

transfer connections (n) Connecting flights providing a continuous journey with passengers' baggage transferred between the flights.

transhumance (n) A traditional event, which involves moving animals such as sheep between different seasonal grazing grounds. Today this is very rare, but it used to take place annually in France and Spain when flocks were moved from their winter quarters to higher summer pastures.

transit (n) The process of being taken or moving between one place to another.

transit passengers (n) Passengers waiting for a connecting flight to their final destination.

translator (n) Person who changes the spoken or written word from one language into another language.

transport 1. (n) Vehicle or craft used to take people or goods from one place to another. **2.** (v) to take people or goods from one place to another.

transport officer (n) Person in charge of travel arrangements or transport.

travel agent (n) Company selling holidays and travel tickets direct to the public on behalf of tour operators and transport companies.

travel agency (n) Retail shop that sells holidays, business travel tickets, and tour packages.

travel document (n) Issued by the Home Office to a person who has no official nationality and therefore no passport. This document allows them to travel internationally but they will have to get a visa for all the countries to which they wish to travel (UK).

travel propensity (n) The proportion of the population that are actively involved in travel.

travel trade manual (n) Book or booklet issued by a tourist board or large hotel group, giving basic information useful when organising tours. Travel trade manuals are issued to the tourism industry only and not to the general public.

traveller (n) Person who goes from one place to another.

traveller's cheque (n) Cheque bought from a bank or travel agent that can easily be exchanged for cash at another bank or bureau de change etc. while travelling abroad. Traveller's cheques are a safe way of carrying money, as issuing banks usually guarantee to replace them if the cheques are stolen. Invented originally by Thomas Cook.

Travicom (n) Air flight information and reservation computer terminal system.

trek (n) Special interest holiday with much of the travelling done on foot or by a form of basic transport such as truck or lorry.

trends (n) The pattern of products that are sold - e.g. the behaviour of customer purchasing which enables a company or organisation to plan future marketing of future products.

trip (n) Journey or tour.

triple (n) Room with three beds.

trolley (n) Small wheeled vehicle used by porters or passengers to transport luggage.

trolley dolly (slang) Term for cabin crew.

tronc (n) Central collection for tips and gratuities in restaurant or hotel.

tropics (n) Area of the world, which normally has warm weather. The tropics are located between the Tropic of Cancer latitude 23° and 30 minutes North, and the Tropic of Capricorn 23° and 30 minutes, South.

tropical rain forest (n) Forests found in the tropical areas of the world which contain a wide variety of plant and animal life. These forests are subject to heavy relief rain during the early mid/part of the afternoon.

T.S. (abbr.) The Tourism Society.

T.S.S.A. (abbr.) Transport Salaried Staffs Association.

T.T.C. (abbr.) The Timeshare Council.

tundra (n) Barren Arctic plains of northern Canada and Eurasia.

turbulence (n) Violent or uneven movement in a particular section of air. This can cause aircraft to be shaken or jolted while in flight.

turn round/around (n) Time allocated

between passengers leaving an aircraft or a ship and it being ready to receive the next group of passengers.

turnover (n) The total income from sales and other receipts that a company earns over a set period of time.

turnpike (n) Toll road (US).

turnstile (n) A metal gateway with revolving central post that will only admit one person at a time.

T.W.B. (abbr.) Twin With Bath. Room with two beds and a bathroom.

twenty-four hour clock (n) System of time measurement which runs from 0001 (12:01am) to 2400 (midnight) each day.

twin (n) Twin room, room with two beds.

twinning (n) When a town forms a social arrangement with another town in another country.

typhoon (n) A violent tropical storm.

Uu - Uniform

U.A.T.P. (abbr.) Universal Air Travel Plan. IATA's credit card facility.

U.D.P. (abbr.) Unitary Development Plan. Proposals that local councils have to submit to Department of the Environment every ten years setting out their plans for tourism and environmental development (UK).

U.F.T.A.A. (abbr.) Universal Federation of Travel Agents' Associations.

U.H.F. (abbr.) Ultra-High Frequency.

U.K. (abbr.) United Kingdom of Great Britain and Northern Ireland.

U.L. (abbr.) Unlicensed (alcohol not served).

U.M. (abbr.) Unaccompanied Minor.

unaccompanied minor (n) Child or young person travelling alone.

unconfirmed (n) Not officially agreed.

undercut (v) Selling goods or services at a lower price than other organisations, usually unofficially.

undercarriage (n) The part of an aircraft that supports it when it is on the ground. This would include the wheels.

underground (n) The name of the London railway system that is situated below the ground.

undertow (n) A current in the sea flowing the opposite way to the surface current, usually away from the shore. Undertow may be dangerous to swimmers as it can pull them out to sea.

UNESCO (acr.) United Nations Educational, Scientific and Cultural Organisation.

Unfair contract terms (n) Legislated act for consumer protection. The Unfair Contract Terms Act 1977 determines the extent to which parties or companies can limit their liability through existing contracts in cases where negligence is proved (UK).

uniform (n) Official clothes provided by an organisation for employees or representatives to wear when working to give a unified image and to make them easily identifiable.

Union Flag (n) Correct name for the flag of the United Kingdom. The term Union Jack should only be used when the flag is flying from a ship.

Unique Selling Point (n) The particular advantage/benefit that one product has said to have over another rival product or competitor.

unlimited (adj.) Without a limit, any amount or quantity is available.

unpressurised (n) When the air inside an aircraft is not pressurised.

upgrade 1. (v) Move to more expensive or superior seats or accommodation. **2.** (n) Seats, accommodation or services of a higher standard are provided at no extra charge.

up-market (n) Term for expensive and/or good quality.

urban (adj.) Living, or situated in a city or town.
usage rate (n) The percentage of facilities being used by customers at different times.
U.S.P. (abbr.) Unique Selling Point - positive aspect of goods or services used in their promotion or marketing.
U.S.T.S. (abbr.) United States Travel Service. Official US agency for promotion of tourism to the USA.

Vv - Victor

V (abbr.) Symbol for vegetarian choice on menu.
vacate (v) Leave accommodation, seat etc. making it available for other people to use.
vacant (adj.) Empty, not being used.
vacancy (n) **1.** Job or position that is available. **2.** Accommodation that is available.
vacation (n) Holiday.
vacationer (n) Holiday-maker (US).
vaccine (n) Substance containing a harmless form of germs that cause a particular disease. This substance is introduced into the body to produce immunity from that particular disease.
vaccination (n) The process of introducing the vaccine into a body, usually by injection.
valet (n) Member of staff in a hotel who looks after the clothes of male guests.
valid (adj.) Acceptable to authority and effective for the intended purpose.
validate (v) To make something valid.
validation (n) Confirmation to ensure something is valid.
validator (n) A mechanical device used to validate a ticket.
validity (n) Period of time for which something is valid.
variable costs (n) The cost of items such as material and labour that change as the volume of business changes.
VAT (abbr.) Value Added Tax.
VAT refund/reclaim (n) Where international passengers can have forms stamped to claim back Value Added Tax.
V.C.R. (abbr.) Video Cassette Recorder.
vehicle (n) Something that is used for transport of people or goods usually on land - i.e. a car, coach, etc..
veld/veldt (n) Wild, uncultivated grassland in South Africa.
ventilate (v) To circulate fresh air.
venue (n) Place that people agree to meet usually that has facilities for conferences, meetings or that has entertainment.
venue inspection (v) Visit made by organisers before an event to check on the facilities etc..
veranda/verandah (n) A raised platform that is situated along the side of a house where people can sit. Some verandas have roofs.
verger (n) A church official in the UK, who could be likened to a 'housekeeper', looking after the church and helping the Vicar in their duties. n.b. At St. Paul's Cathedral (London, UK) they are called Virgers.
verify (v) To check or confirm that something is accurate or correct.
vertical integration (n) When a company merges or purchases another company that is involved in a different stage of producing or distributing the same type of product.
V.F.R. (abbr.) Visiting Friends and Relatives.
V.H.F. (abbr.) Very High Frequency. Radio broadcasting frequency between 30 - 300 MHz.
via **1.** (preposition) To go through a place on the way to a destination. **2.** (n) Italian for road.
viability (n) The chances of a business succeeding.

viaduct (n) Bridge of short spans supported on piers or towers, that carries a railway or road across a valley.

vicar (n) The priest of a parish; a church official who takes church services and administers to the needs of the local people (UK).

vice versa (preposition) The other or opposite way round to that which has been stated.

video cassette (n) A sealed cartridge containing magnetic tape (video tape) used for recording sounds and pictures. These sounds and pictures can to be shown on a television using a video player.

video conferencing (n) System using video cameras connected by telephone lines, enabling people to see and talk to each other, even if they are separated by a long distance.

video player (n) Equipment which plays or reads video cassettes or tapes and displays sounds and pictures stored on them on a television or monitor.

video recorder (n) Equipment for recording sounds and pictures on to video cassettes or tape.

video tape (n) Long flexible Magnetic strip (tape) used for recording sounds and pictures which can later be played back or read using a video player.

videowall (n) A large display made up of video screens.

view line (n) Eye level of each member of the audience, in relation to the stage.

villa (n) Large house, usually a house where people stay while on holiday.

village (n) Small settlement or collection of houses, generally with a church and shops.

V.I.P. (abbr.) Very Important Person.

virtual reality (n) A three dimensional computer simulation of a place or object, usually viewed through a headset.

visa (n) Official stamp or paper in a passport, to show the holder can enter or leave a foreign country.

visibles/visible assets (n) Income received by a country from trading in goods rather than services. Visible assets include manufactured items and food. Services are counted as invisible assets.

visibility (n) The distance which the light or weather allows people to see.

visit 1. (v) To go to a place, venue or country for a short time (not permanently) for the purposes of pleasure or business. **2.** (n) The period of time or act of visiting.

visitor (n) Person who goes to a place, venue or country for a short time (not permanently) for the purposes of pleasure or business.

visitor attraction (n) Venue opened for tourist visits.

visitor centre (n) Reception area that gives visitors tourist information about a geographical area, museum or other place of interest.

visitor payback (n) A levy, usually voluntary, added to a bill which tourists contribute to conserving the place they are visiting.

visitor profile (n) Description of an average customer - e.g. lifestyle.

vocational qualification (n) Non academic qualification that is usually obtained in the workplace.

volcano (n) Mountain through which molten lava, gas, ash etc. from under the surface of the earth bursts out or erupts. Volcanoes can be dormant or 'dead' and so are unlikely to erupt.

volume (n) The amount or quantity of something - i.e. volume of traffic or sound.

voluntary sector (n) Organisations funded by people on a voluntary basis.

voucher (n) Ticket given as a receipt for payment which the holder can use instead of money to obtain specified goods or services.

Voyage (n) Journey on a ship.

V.S.T.O.L. (abbr.) Vertical Short Takeoff and Landing aircraft.

V.T.O.L. (abbr.) Vertical Takeoff and Landing aircraft.

V.V. (abbr.) Vice versa.

V.V.V. (abbr.) Tourist Information Centres in the Netherlands.

Ww - Whisky

wadi (n) Valley, stream or riverbed in the Middle East which is usually dry, but after rain becomes the main channel for water.

Wagons-Lit (n) Name of the company that operates sleeping accommodation on European trains.

wait listed (adj.) Passengers on a waiting list for an aircraft flight that is already fully booked.

waiter (n) Man employed to serve customers food at their table in a restaurant.

waitress (n) Woman employed to serve customers food at their table in a restaurant.

wake up call (n) See Alarm call.

walkie talkie (slang) The slang term for a short range two way radio.

walking tour (n) Guided tour travelling by or on foot.

warden (n) An official in a National Park, National Trust property etc..

Warsaw Convention (n) Convention held in 1929 to establish an agreement on the extent of liability for death, injury or loss of luggage that an airline has to its passengers. The Warsaw Convention currently limits compensation payments to relatively low amounts, however, moves are being made to raise the limit.

W.A.T.A. (abbr.) World Association of Travel Agencies.

water park (n) Recreation area with water sports and other water based activities.

water taxi (n) Small motor boat used to transport people.

waybill (n) List of goods or passengers being transported.

weekend (n) Days at the end of the working week when businesses are normally shut.

weekend break (n) Short holiday the duration of which is a weekend.

weekend surcharge (n) An extra charge for travellers between specified times at a weekend.

welcome (n) To greet in a friendly way.

welcome cocktail (n) Drinks served to visitors on their arrival so that they can all meet each other.

Welcome Host (n) Customer Care training programme for hotels, guesthouses, restaurants, and any staff from organisations and shops that are in contact with tourists. The programme aims to raise the standards of hospitality and service.

welcome meeting (n) Where a tour operators' representatives (Reps.) welcome clients to a resort, give them an introduction to the resort and what activities and excursions are available.

wet hire (n) When equipment for an exhibition or conference is hired with operators/technicians.

wet lease (n) Where an aircraft is leased with crew.

wetland (n) Marsh or damp uncultivated land.

WH (abbr.) Western Hemisphere.

wharf (n) Platform or structure next to a river or to the sea where ships berth. Often used as an loading/unloading area for passengers and cargo.

whispered interpreting (n) Simultaneous interpreting in a low voice to one or two persons seated adjacent to the interpreter.

white board (n) A shiny white board on which a lecturer or speaker can draw or write using special pens, so that the board can be cleaned afterwards.
white knuckle ride (n) Very exciting rides such as Roller Coasters. These are determined by speed, height etc..
white tie (adj.) This refers to a white bow tie worn by men at an event requiring formal clothing and a long evening dress for women. See also black tie.
white water rafting (n) A boat ride along a stretch of shallow and foamy water, usually involving navigation around rocks.
W.H.O. (abbr.) World Health Organisation.
wholesaler (n) **1.** Tour operator - often one who sells to companies and not directly to the public. **2.** commercial organisation that sell goods at a discount to retailers.
wide-bodied jet (n) Air/aeroplane with extra wide body that has more seats than a normal air/aeroplane.
wildlife park (n) Place where animals are kept in simulated natural surroundings and can be viewed by the public.
wind-chill factor (n) The cooling effect of wind.
windsurfer (n) **1.** A board similar to a surfboard with a sail. **2.** Person who sails a windsurfer on water.
wine waiter (n) Waiter who serves wine to customers in a restaurant.
wings (n) **1.** The long flat parts of an aircraft that stick out of the side and provide lift that support it while in flight. The engines are usually attached to them. **2.** The part of a building that sticks out from the main part - usually associated with large houses, hospitals etc.. **3.** The part of the stage that is hidden from the audience - theatres, conferences etc..
W/L (abbr.) Wait Listed.
W.L. (abbr.) Waiting List.
working capital (n) Money that is used to buy stock and other non capital items when starting a business.
workshop (n) **1.** Meetings, usually held around small tables, to enable participants to share their knowledge and experience through a series of discussions and practical work. **2.** Place where craftsmen work which contains their tools etc..
world heritage site (n) UNESCO defined sites of natural, historical, or conservational importance around the world.
Worldspan (n) CRS system (airlines).
W.T.B. (abbr.) Wales Tourist Board.
W.T.C. (abbr.) World Tourism Council.
W.T.O. (abbr.) World Tourism Organisation.
W.T.T.C. (abbr.) World Travel and Tourism Council.

Xx - X-ray

xenophobia (n) Strong dislike or fear of foreigners or non-natives.
Xmas (abbr.) Christmas.
X.O. (abbr.) Exchange Order.
X-ray (n) Radiation that can pass through most solid materials. Machines that use X-rays are used to check the contents of luggage, especially at airports, for illegal or dangerous goods. X-rays are also used to examine broken bones and other internal injuries.

Yy - Yankee

Y (abbr.) Economy Class.
yacht (n) Boat or small sailing ship.
yellow card (n) Internationally acknowledged record of vaccination and immunisation against disease.
Yen (n) Japanese unit of currency.
Y.H.A. (abbr.) Youth Hostel Association.
Y.M.C.A. (abbr.) Young Men's Christian Association. A hostel for men administered

by the Y.M.C.A..

youth (n) Young person, usually less than 26 years old.

youth hostel (n) Inexpensive accommodation, that often includes dormitories, for young people or those travelling on a small budget.

Y.W.C.A. (abbr.) Young Women's Christian Association. A hostel administered by the Y.W.C.A. organisation where women can stay.

Zz - Zulu

Z (abbr.) Used to Signify time in Greenwich Mean Time (G.M.T.).

zero (n) Naught, nil, null or 0.

zero-rated (n) No tax applies to items which are zero rated - i.e. no VAT payable (UK).

zone (n) **1.** A defined area of earth's surface - i.e. time-zone. **2.** A defined area such as secure area of an airport.

zoo (n) Display of animals that is open to the public.

Conference Seating Arrangements

1. Theatre style seating

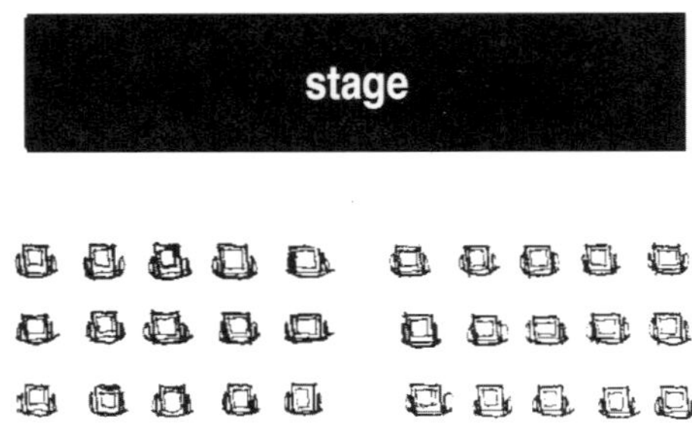

2. Classroom style seating

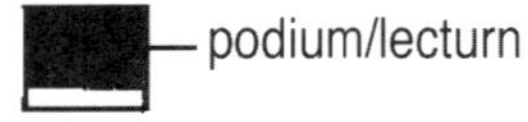

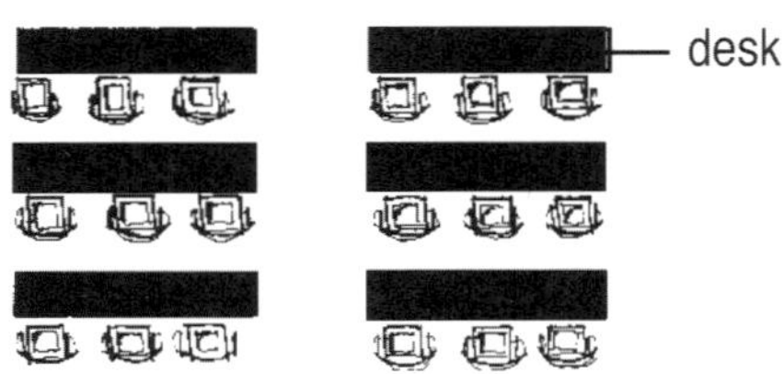

3. Boardroom style seating

Manually Issued Airline Ticket

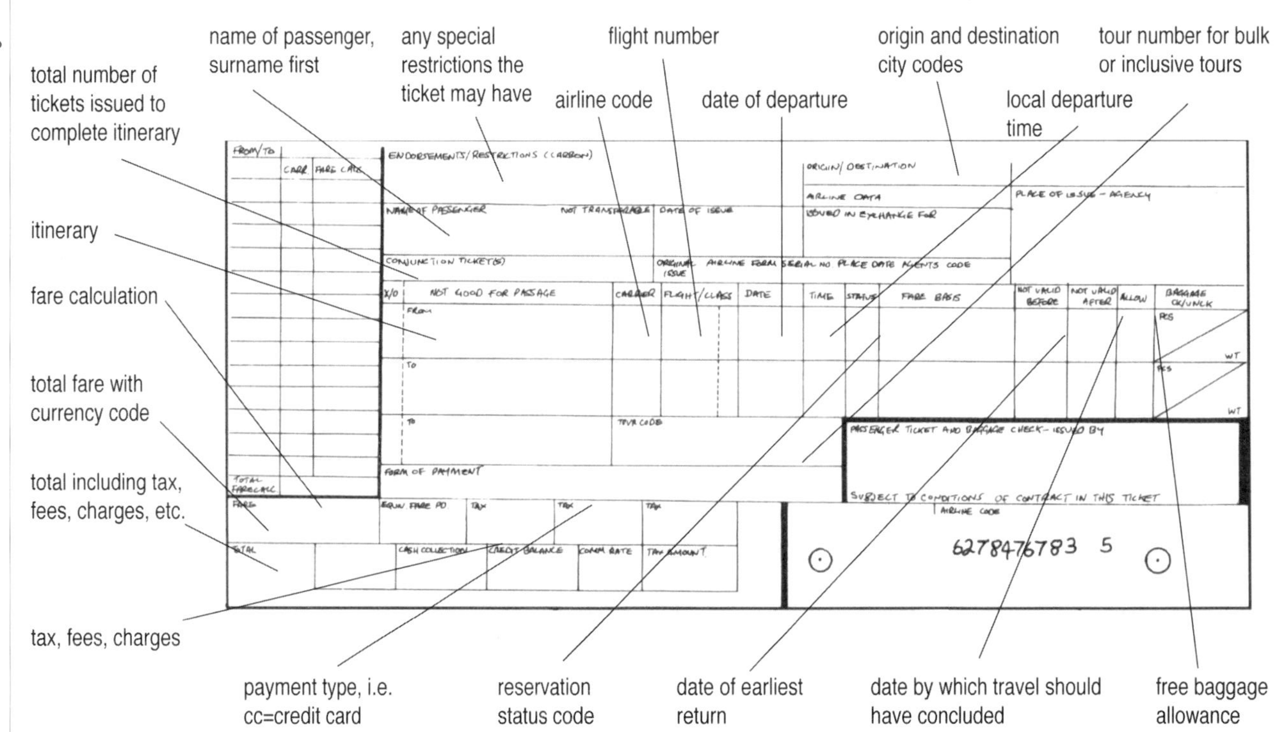

Automated Airline Ticket

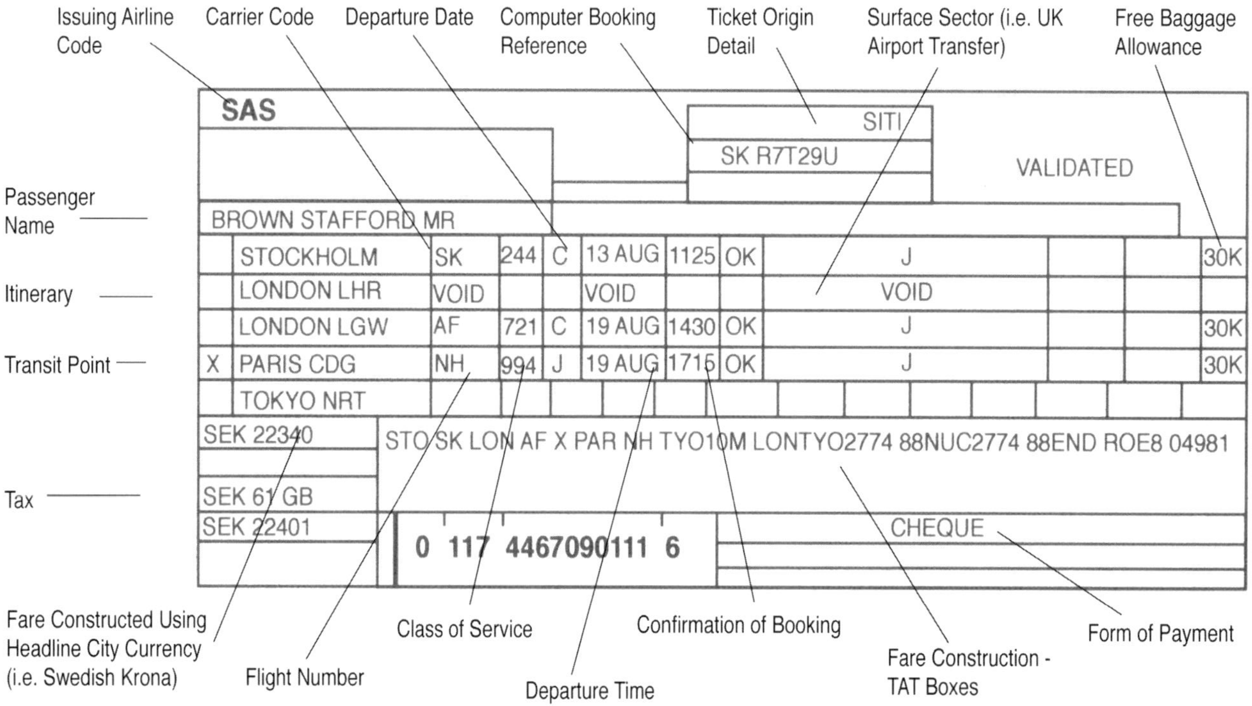

Issuing Airline Code

Carrier Code

Departure Date

Computer Booking Reference

Ticket Origin Detail

Surface Sector (i.e. UK Airport Transfer)

Free Baggage Allowance

SAS

SITI

SK R7T29U

VALIDATED

Passenger Name — BROWN STAFFORD MR

Itinerary

Transit Point

	STOCKHOLM	SK	244	C	13 AUG	1125	OK	J	30K
	LONDON LHR	VOID			VOID			VOID	
	LONDON LGW	AF	721	C	19 AUG	1430	OK	J	30K
X	PARIS CDG	NH	994	J	19 AUG	1715	OK	J	30K
	TOKYO NRT								

SEK 22340

STO SK LON AF X PAR NH TYO10M LONTYO2774 88NUC2774 88END ROE8 04981

Tax — SEK 61 GB

SEK 22401

0 117 4467090111 6

CHEQUE

Fare Constructed Using Headline City Currency (i.e. Swedish Krona)

Flight Number

Class of Service

Departure Time

Confirmation of Booking

Fare Construction - TAT Boxes

Form of Payment

Countries of the World

AFGHANISTAN
Capital - Kabul
Language.- Pushtu, Dari
Currency - Afghani
Religion - Muslim, Sunni (Persian)
Climate - Continental
Int. Dialling Code - Int.+ 93

ALBANIA
Capital - Tirana
Language - Albanian, Greek
Currency - Lek
Religion - Muslim
Climate - Mediterranean
Int. Dialling Code - Int. + 355

ALGERIA
Capital - Algiers
Language - Arabic, Berber, French
Currency - Dinar
Religion - Muslim
Climate - South of Country is very hot, North (Coast) Mediterranean
Int. Dialling Code - Int. + 213

ANDORRA
Capital - Andorra-la-Vella
Language - French, Spanish
Currencies - French Franc, Spanish Paseta
Religion - Roman Catholic
Climate - Winter is severe, Summer is cool and sunny
Int. Dialling Code - Int. + 33628

ANGOLA
Capital - Luanda
Language - Portuguese and African Languages
Currency - Kwanza
Religion - Roman Catholic, Protestant
Climate - Tropical
Int. Dialling Code - Int. + 244

ANTIGUA AND BARBUDA
Capital - St. John's
Language - English
Currency - East Caribbean Dollar
Religion - Christian
Climate - Tropical
Int. Dialling Code - Int. + 1809
UK Tourist Office - 020 7486 7073/5

ARGENTINA
Capital - Buenos Aires
Language - Spanish (Official), English, French, Italian, German
Currency - Peso
Religion - Roman Catholic
Climate - North is subtropical, South is subarctic
Int. Dialling Code - Int. + 54

AUSTRALIA
Capital - Canberra
Language - English
Currency - Australian Dollar
Religion - Anglican, Roman Catholic, Protestant
Climate - Hot and Dry
Int. Dialling Code - Int. + 61
UK Tourist Office - 020 8780 2229

AUSTRIA
Capital - Vienna
Language - German
Currency - Schilling
Religion - Roman Catholic, Protestant
Climate - Continental
Int. Dialling Code - Int. + 43
UK Tourist Office - 020 7629 0461

BAHAMAS
Capital - Nassau
Language - English, Caribbean Creole
Currency - Bahamian Dollar
Religion - Anglican, Baptist, Roman Catholic
Climate - Subtropical and Mild
Int. Dialling Code - Int. + 1809
UK Tourist Office - 01483 448 900

BAHRAIN
Capital - Manama
Language - Arabic (Official), English, Farsi, Urdu
Currency - Bahrain Dinar
Religion - Muslim
Climate - Very Dry, Very Hot in Summer and also very humid
Int. Dialling Code - Int. + 973

BANGLADESH
Capital - Dhaka
Language - Bengali, English
Currency - Taka
Religions - Sunni Muslim, Hindu
Climate - Tropical
Int. Dialling Code - Int. + 880

BARBADOS
Capital - Bridgetown
Language - English
Currency - Barbados Dollar
Religion - Anglican
Climate - Subtropical
Int. Dialling Code - Int. + 1809
UK Tourist Office - 020 7636 9448

BELGIUM
Capital - Brussels
Language - Flemish in the north of the country, Walloon (French) in the south of the country
Currency - Belgian Franc
Religion - Roman Catholic
Climate - Temperate
Int. Dialling Code - Int. + 32
UK Tourist Office - 020 7629 3977

BOLIVIA
Capital - La Paz
Language - Spanish and Local Languages
Currency - Boliviano
Religion - Roman Catholic
Climate - Tropical, cooler on higher ground
Int. Dialling Code - Int. + 591

BOTSWANA
Capital - Gabarone
Language - English, Setswana
Currency - Pula
Religion - Christian, Tribal
Climate - Subtropical and Dry
Int. Dialling Code - Int. + 267

BRAZIL
Capital - Brasillia
Language - Portuguese and numerous Indian Languages
Currency - Real
Religion - Roman Catholic
Climate - Tropical and Subtropical
Int. Dialling Code - Int. + 55
UK Tourist Office - 020 7499 0877

BRUNEI
Capital - Bandar Seri Begawan
Language - Mostly Malay (Official), Chinese, English
Currency - Brunei Dollar
Religion - Muslim, Confucianist, Buddhist, Taoist
Climate - Tropical - very humid and wet
Int. Dialling Code - Int. + 673

BULGARIA
Capital - Sofia
Language - Bulgarian, Turkish
Currency - Lev
Religion - Eastern Orthodox Christian
Climate - Continental in north of country

and in the mountains, Mediterranean in the south.
Int. Dialling Code - Int. + 359

CAMBODIA
Capital - Phnom Penh
Language - Khmer (Official), French
Currency - Cambodian Riel
Religion - Therevada Buddhist
Climate - Tropical. Monsoon from April to October.
Int. Dialling Code - Int + 855

CAMEROON
Capital - Yaounde
Language - French, English, Tribal (Various African Languages)
Currency - African Financial Community Franc
Religion - Roman Catholic, Muslim, Tribal (Various African Religions)
Climate - Tropical
Int. Dialling Code - Int. + 237

CANADA
Capital - Ottawa
Language - English, French
Currency - Canadian Dollar
Religion - Roman Catholic, Protestant
Climate - Continental, Arctic in the north
Int. Dialling Code - Int. + 1
UK Tourist Office - 020 7930 8540

CHILE
Capital - Santiago
Language - Spanish
Currency - Peso
Religion - Roman Catholic
Climate - Desert in the north, Arctic in the south
Int. Dialling Code - Int. + 56

CHINA
Capital - Beijing
Language - Chinese (Mandarin-official, Cantonese and variations of these two dialects)
Currency - Yuan
Religion - Confucianist, Muslim, Taoist, Buddhist
Climate - Temperate and Humid in the south and the central south. Dry in the north.
Int. Dialling Code - Int. + 86
UK Tourist Office - 020 7935 9787

COLOMBIA
Capital - Bogota
Language - Spanish
Currency - Peso
Religion - Roman Catholic
Climate - Tropical, Temperate on the plateaux
Int. Dialling Code - Int. + 57

COSTA RICA
Capital - San Jose
Language - Spanish
Currency - Colon
Religion - Roman Catholic
Climate - Tropical, Temperate on the plateaux
Int. Dialling Code - Int. + 506

CROATIA
Capital - Zagreb
Language - Croatian variant of Serbo-Croatian
Currency - Croatian Dinar
Religion - Roman Catholic (Croats), Orthodox Christian (Serbs)
Climate - Continental in the north, Mediterranean in the south.
Int. Dialling Code - Int. + 385
UK Tourist Office - 020 8563 7979

CUBA
Capital - Havana
Language - Spanish
Currency - Cuban Peso

Religion - Roman Catholic
Climate - Subtropical
Int. Dialling Code - Int. + 53
UK Tourist Office - 020 7379 1706

CYPRUS
Capital - Larnaca
Language - Greek and Turkish (Official), English
Currencies - Cyprus Pound, Turkish Lira
Religion - Greek Orthodox
Climate - Mediterranean
Int. Dialling Code - Int. + 357
UK Tourist Office - 020 7734 9822

CZECH REPUBLIC
Capital - Prague
Language - Czech
Currency - The new Krown / Koruna
Religion - Mainly Roman Catholic
Climate - Continental - hot summers and cold winters
Int. Dialling Code - Int. + 42

DENMARK
Capital - Copenhagen
Language - Danish
Currency - Kroner
Religion - Lutheran
Climate - Maritime
Int. Dialling Code - Int. + 45
UK Tourist Office - 020 7259 5959

DOMINICA
Capital - Roseau
Language - English
Currencies - East Caribbean Dollar, Pound Sterling, French Franc
Religion - Roman Catholic
Climate - Subtropical
Int. Dialling Code - Int. + 1809
UK Tourist Office - 020 7835 1937

DOMINICAN REPUBLIC
Capital - Santo Domingo
Language - Spanish
Currency - Peso
Religion - Roman Catholic
Climate - Subtropical and Maritime Tropical
Int. Dialling Code - Int. + 1809

ECUADOR
Capital - Quito
Language - Spanish, Various Indian Languages
Currency - Sucre
Religion - Roman Catholic
Climate - Tropical, cooler on higher ground
Int. Dialling Code - Int. + 593

EGYPT
Capital - Cairo
Language - Arabic
Currency - Egyptian Pound
Religion - Muslim
Climate - Hot an Dry
Int. Dialling Code - Int. + 20
UK Tourist Office - 020 7493 5282

EL SALVADOR
Capital - San Salvador
Language - Spanish
Currency - Colon
Religion - Roman Catholic
Climate - Subtropical, much cooler on the higher ground
Int. Dialling Code - Int. + 503

ESTONIA
Capital - Tallinn
Language - Estonian (Finnish extraction)
Currency - Kroon
Religion - Lutheran
Climate - Temperate, cold winters
Int. Dialling Code - Int. + 372

ETHIOPIA
Capital - Addis Ababa
Language - Amharic

Currency - Birr
Religion - Ethiopian Christian, Sunni Muslim
Climate - Hot on the low ground, Temperate on the higher Ground
Int. Dialling Code - Int. + 251

FIJI
Capital - Suva
Language - English (Official), Hindi, Fijian
Currency - Fiji Dollar
Religion - Hindu, Methodist
Climate - Tropical
Int. Dialling Code - Int. + 679
UK Tourist Office - 020 8392 1838

FINLAND
Capital - Helsinki
Language - Finnish and Swedish
Currency - Markka
Religion - Lutheran
Climate - Temperate, very cold winters
Int. Dialling Code - Int. + 358
UK Tourist Office - 020 7839 4048

FRANCE
Capital - Paris
Language - French
Currency - French Franc
Religion - Roman Catholic
Climate - Temperate, Dry and Hot summers on the Mediterranean coast - the south of the country
Int. Dialling Code - Int. + 33
UK Tourist Office - 0891 244123

GABON
Capital - Libreville
Language - French (Official), various African languages
Currency - African Financial Community Franc - CFA Franc
Religion - Christian
Climate - Tropical
Int. Dialling Code - Int. + 241

GAMBIA
Capital - Banjul
Languages - English (Official), Various African Languages
Currency - Dalasi
Religion - Muslim
Climate - Tropical
Int. Dialling Code - Int. + 220
UK Tourist Office - 020 7736 0093

GERMANY
Capital - Berlin
Language - German
Currency - Deutsche mark
Religion - Protestant, Roman Catholic
Climate - Continental - Temperate
Int. Dialling Code - Int. + 49
UK Tourist Office - 020 7495 0081

GHANA
Capital - Accra
Language - English (Official), various African languages
Currency - Cedi
Religion - Christian, Muslim, Tribal-various African religions
Climate - Tropical
Int. Dialling Code - Int. + 233
UK Tourist Office - 020 7493 4901

GREECE
Capital - Athens
Language - Greek
Currency - Drachma
Religion - Greek Orthodox
Climate - Mediterranean
Int. Dialling Code - Int. + 30
UK Tourist Office - 020 7734 5997

GRENADA
Capital - St. George's
Language - English
Currency - East Caribbean Dollar
Religion - Christian, Roman Catholic
Climate - Subtropical

Int. Dialling Code - Int. + 1809
UK Tourist Office - 020 7370 5164/5

GUATEMALA
Capital - Guatemala City
Language - Spanish, various Indian languages.
Currency - Quetzal
Religion - Roman Catholic, Protestant
Climate - Subtropical, Temperate on the higher ground
Int. Dialling Code - Int. + 502

GUYANA
Capital - Georgetown
Language - English (Official), Hindi, Urdu, various local languages
Currency - Guyanese Dollar
Religion - Christian, Hindu, Urdu
Climate - Tropical
Int. Dialling Code - Int. + 592

HAITI
Capital - Port-au-Prince
Language - French, Creole-Caribbean English
Currency - Gourde
Religion - Christian, Voodoo
Climate - Tropical
Int. Dialling Code - Int. + 509

HONDURAS
Capital - Tegucigalpa
Language - Spanish (Official), English, various Indian languages
Currency - Lempira
Religion - Roman Catholic
Climate - Tropical
Int. Dialling Code - Int. + 504

HONG KONG
Capital - Victoria
Language - English, Chinese
Currency - Hong Kong Dollar
Religion - Buddhist, Taoist
Climate - Subtropical, monsoon season from May to September
Int. Dialling Code - Int. +852
UK Tourist Office - 020 7930 4775

HUNGARY
Capital - Budapest
Language - Hungarian (Magyar)
Currency - Forint
Religion - Roman Catholic
Climate - Continental
Int. Dialling Code - Int. + 36
UK Tourist Office - 020 8871 4009

ICELAND
Capital - Reykjavik
Language - Icelandic
Currency - Krona
Religion - Lutheran
Climate - Temperate
Int. Dialling Code - Int. + 354
UK Tourist Office - 020 7388 7550

INDIA
Capital - New Delhi
Language - Hindi, English, also numerous other languages such as Bengali, Urdu, Tamil, Punjabi
Currency - Rupee
Religion - Hindu. Also numerous other religions such as Muslim, Sikh, Christian, Buddhist, Jain
Climate - Tropical, monsoon season from June to September.
Int. Dialling Code - Int. + 91
UK Tourist Office - 020 7437 3677

INDONESIA
Capital - Jakarta
Languages - Indonesian
Currency - Rupiah
Religion - Muslim, also Christian, Buddhist, Hindu
Climate - Equatorial
Int. Dialling Code - Int. +62

UK Tourist Office - 020 7439 0030

IRAN
Capital - Tehran
Language - Farsi (Official)
Currency - Rial
Religion - Shi'ite Muslim (Official)
Climate - Continental
Int. Dialling Code - Int. + 98

IRAQ
Capital - Baghdad
Language - Arabic (Official), also Kurdish, Turkish, Assyrian
Currency - Iraqi Dinar
Religion - Muslim
Climate - Very Hot Summers, cool winters
Int. Dialling Code - Int. + 964

IRELAND
Capital - Dublin
Language - English, Irish Gaelic (Both Official)
Currency - Punt
Religion - Roman Catholic
Climate - Temperate
Int. Dialling Code - Int. + 353
UK Tourist Office - 020 7518 0800

ISRAEL
Capital - Jerusalem
Language - Hebrew and Arabic (Both Official)
Currency - Shekel
Religion - Judaism
Climate - Subtropical
Int. Dialling Code - Int. + 972
UK Tourist Office - 020 7636 9448

ITALY
Capital - Rome
Language - Italian
Currency - Lira
Religion - Roman Catholic
Climate - Mediterranean
Int. Dialling Code - Int. + 39
UK Tourist Office - 020 7408 1254

JAMAICA
Capital - Kingston
Language - English, Spanish, Jamaican Creole
Currency - Jamaican Dollar
Religion - Roman Catholic, Rastafarian
Climate - Tropical on sea level, temperate on higher ground (mountains)
Int. Dialling Code - Int. + 1809
UK Tourist Office - 020 7224 0505

JAPAN
Capital - Tokyo
Language - Japanese
Currency - Yen
Religion - Shinto, Buddhist - Shintoism, Christian
Climate - Monsoon climate
Int. Dialling Code - Int. + 81
UK Tourist Office - 020 7734 9638

JORDAN
Capital - Amman
Languages - Arabic (Official), English
Currency - Jordanian Dinar
Religion - Sunni Muslim, Christian
Climate - Hot and Dry, cool in the winter.
Int. Dialling Code - Int. + 962
UK Tourist Office - 020 7437 9465

KENYA
Capital - Nairobi
Language - Swahilli (Official), English and various African languages
Currency - Kenya Shilling
Religion - Christian, various African Muslim religions
Climate - Tropical, temperate inland
Int. Dialling Code - Int. + 254
UK Tourist Office - 020 7355 3144/45
KOREA, NORTH
Capital - Pyongyang

Language - Korean
Currency - Won
Religion - Buddhist, Confucianist
Climate - Continental
Int. Dialling Code - Int. + 850

KOREA, SOUTH
Capital - Seoul
Language - Korean
Currency - Won
Religion - Buddhist, Christian, Confucianist
Climate - Continental
Int. Dialling Code - Int + 82
UK Tourist Office - 020 7408 1591

KUWAIT
Capital - Kuwait City
Language - Arabic, Farsi, Kurdish, English
Currency - Kuwaiti Dinar
Religion - Muslim
Climate - Hot and Dry
Int. Dialling Code - Int. + 965

LAOS
Capital - Vientiane
Languages - Lao (Official), French
Currency - New Kip
Religion - Buddhist
Climate - Tropical, monsoon season May to October
Int. Dialling Code - Int. + 856

LEBANON
Capital - Beirut
Language - Arabic, French (Both Official), English, Armenian
Currency - Lebanese Pound
Religions - Muslim, Christian
Climate - Subtropical
Int. Dialling Code - Int. + 961
UK Tourist Office - 020 7409 2031

LESOTHO
Capital - Maseru
Language - English, Sesotho (Both Official), Zulu, Xhosa
Currency - Maluti
Religion - Protestant, Roman Catholic
Climate - Continental
Int. Dialling Code - Int. + 266

LIBYA
Capital - Tripoli
Language - Arabic
Currency - Libyan Dinar
Religion - Muslim
Climate - Hot and Dry
Int. Dialling Code - Int. + 218

LIECHTENSTEIN
Capital - Vaduz
Language - German
Currency - Swiss Franc
Religion - Roman Catholic, Protestant
Climate - Temperate
Int. Dialling Code - Int. + 4175

LUXEMBOURG
Capital - Luxembourg City
Language - French (Official), German, Letzeburgesh - A spoken language, not a written language.
Currency - Luxembourg Franc
Religion - Roman Catholic
Climate - Temperate
Int. Dialling Code - Int. + 352
UK Tourist Office - 020 7434 2800

MADAGASCAR
Capital - Antananarivo
Languages - Malagasy (Official), French, English
Currency - Malagasy Franc
Religion - Tribal- various religions, Christian, Muslim
Climate - Tropical
Int. Dialling Code - Int. + 261
MALAYSIA
Capital - Kuala Lumpar

Languages - Malay (Official),
Currency - Rinngit
Religion - Muslim (Official), Buddhist
Climate - Tropical, monsoon season from October to February in the east, monsoon season from May to September in the west.
Int. Dialling Code - Int. + 60
UK Tourist Office - 020 7930 7932

MALDIVES
Capital - Male
Languages - Divehi - Sinhalese Dialect, English
Currency - Rufiya
Religion - Muslim
Climate - Tropical, monsoon season from June to August
Int. Dialling Code - Int. + 960
UK Tourist Office - 020 7352 2246

MALTA
Capital - Valletta
Language - English, Maltese
Currency - Maltese Lira
Religion - Roman Catholic
Climate - Mediterranean
Int. Dialling Code - Int. + 356
UK Tourist Office - 020 7292 4900

MAURITIUS
Capital - Port Louis
Language - English (Official), French, Creole, various Indian languages
Currency - Mauritius Rupee
Religion - Hindu, Christian, Muslim
Climate - Subtropical
Int. Dialling Code - Int. + 230
UK Tourist Office - 020 7584 3666

MEXICO
Capital - Mexico City
Language - Spanish (Official)
Currency - Peso
Religion - Roman Catholic
Climate - Tropical on lower ground, Temperate on higher ground
Int. Dialling Code - Int. + 52
UK Tourist Office - 020 77345 1058

MONACO
Capital - Monaco-Ville
Language - French (Official)
Currency - French Franc
Religion - Roman Catholic
Climate - Mediterranean
Int. Dialling Code - Int. + 3393
UK Tourist Office - 020 7352 9962

MONGOLIA
Capital - Ulan Bator
Language - Mongolian (Official), Chinese, Russian
Currency - Tugrik
Religion - Buddhist, but officially none
Climate - Dry and Cold
Int. Dialling Code - Int. + 976

MOROCCO
Capital - Rabat
Language - Arabic (Official), Berber, French, Spanish
Currency - Dirham
Religion - Muslim
Climate - Warm
Int. Dialling Code - Int. + 212
UK Tourist Office - 020 7437 0073

MYANMAR - Formerly known as Burma
Capital - Yangon - Formerly known as Rangoon
Language - Burmese
Currency - Kyat
Religion - Buddhist
Climate - Tropical, monsoon season from May to September
Int. Dialling Code - Int. + 95

NAMIBIA
Capital - Windhoek

Language - Afrikaans, English, German, also several other African languages
Currency - South African - Rand
Religion - Lutheran, Roman Catholic, Christian
Climate - Very Dry
Int. Dialling Code - Int. + 264
UK Tourist Office - 020 7636 2924

NEPAL
Capital - Katmandu
Language - Nepali (Official), numerous other local languages
Currency - Nepalese Rupee
Religion - Hindu
Climate - Temperate
Int. Dialling Code - Int. + 977

NETHERLANDS
Capital - Amsterdam
Language - Dutch
Currency - Guilder
Religion - Roman Catholic, Protestant
Climate - Temperate
Int. Dialling Code - Int. + 31
UK Tourist Office - 0891 200277

NEW ZEALAND
Capital - Wellington
Language - English (Official), Maori
Currency - New Zealand Dollar
Religion - Protestant, Roman Catholic
Climate - Temperate
Int. Dialling Code - Int. + 64
UK Tourist Office - 0839 300900

NICARAGUA
Capital - Managua
Language - Spanish (Official), Indian, English
Currency - Cordoba
Religion - Roman Catholic
Climate - Tropical
Int. Dialling Code - Int. + 505

NIGERIA
Capital - Lagos
Language - English (Official), Hausu, Ibo, Yoruba
Currency - Naira
Religion - Muslim, Christian
Climate - Subtropical
Int. Dialling Code - Int. + 234

NORWAY
Capital - Oslo
Language - Norwegian (Official)
Currency - Krone
Religion - Lutheran
Climate - Temperate, cold in the north of the country
Int. Dialling Code - Int. + 47
UK Tourist Office - 020 7839 6255

OMAN
Capital - Muscat
Language - Arabic (Official), English
Currency - Rial Omani
Religion - Muslim
Climate - Hot summer, Mild winter
Int. Dialling Code - Int. + 968

PAKISTAN
Capital - Islamabad
Language - Urdu and English (Both Official), Punjabi, other languages as well
Currency - Pakistan Rupee
Religion - Muslim
Climate - Subtropical, monsoon season from June to October
Int. Dialling Code - Int. + 92

PANAMA
Capital - Panama City
Language - Spanish (Official), English
Currency - Balboa
Religion - Roman Catholic
Climate - Tropical
Int. Dialling Code - Int. + 507

PAPUA NEW GUINEA
Capital - Port Moresby
Language - English (Official), Tok Pisin-Pidgin English, literally hundreds of other languages-700 approx.
Currency - Kina
Religion - Christian
Climate - Tropical
Int. Dialling Code - Int. + 675
UK Tourist Office - 020 8392 1838

PARAGUAY
Capital - Ascuncion
Language - Spanish (Official), Guarani
Currency - Guarani
Religion - Roman Catholic
Climate - Subtropical
Int. Dialling Code - Int. + 595

PERU
Capital - Lima
Language - Spanish, Quechua (Both Official)
Currency - New Sol
Religion - Roman Catholic
Climate - Temperate, cooler on higher ground
Int. Dialling Code - Int. + 51
UK Tourist Office - 020 7235 2545

PHILIPPINES
Capital - Manila
Language - Tagalog-Philipino (Official), English, Spanish
Currency - Philippine Peso
Religion - Roman Catholic
Climate - Tropical
Int. Dialling Code - Int. + 63
UK Tourist Office - 020 7499 5443

POLAND
Capital - Warsaw
Language - Polish (Official), German
Currency - Zloty
Religion - Roman Catholic
Climate - Temperate
Int. Dialling Code - Int. + 48
UK Tourist Office - 020 7580 8811

PORTUGAL
Capital - Lisbon
Language - Portuguese
Currency - Escudo
Religion - Roman Catholic
Climate - Hot and Dry summers, mild and damp winters
Int. Dialling Code - Int. + 351
UK Tourist Office - 020 7494 1441

PUERTO RICO
Capital - San Juan
Language - Spanish, English
Currency - U.S. Dollar
Religion - Roman Catholic
Climate - Subtropical
Int. Dialling Code - Int. + 1809

QATAR
Capital - Doha
Language - Arabic (Official), English
Currency - Qatar Riyal
Religion - Muslim
Climate - Hot, cooler in the winter
Int. Dialling Code - Int. + 974

ROMANIA
Capital - Bucharest
Language - Romanian
Currency - Leu
Religion - Romanian Orthodox
Climate - Continental
Int. Dialling Code - Int. + 40
UK Tourist Office - 020 7224 3692

RUSSIA
Capital - Moscow
Language - Russian
Currency - Rouble
Religion - Mainly Russian Orthodox
Climate - Continental, arctic in the north

Int. Dialling Code - Int. + 7
UK Tourist Office - 0891 516951

ST. LUCIA
Capital - Castries
Language - English, French Patois
Currency - East Caribbean Dollar
Religion - Roman Catholic
Climate - Subtropical
Int. Dialling Code - Int. + 1809
UK Tourist Office - 020 7431 3675

ST. VINCENT AND THE GRENADINES
Capital - Kingston
Language - English, French Patois
Currency - East Caribbean Dollar
Religion - Christian
Climate - Subtropical, dry season January to May
Int. Dialling Code - Int. + 1809
UK Tourist Office - 020 7937 6570

SAN MARINO
Capital - San Marino
Language - Italian
Currency - Italian Lira
Religion - Roman Catholic
Climate - Mediterranean
Int. Dialling Code - Int. + 39549

SAUDI ARABIA
Capital - Riyadh
Language - Arabic
Currency - Rial
Religion - Muslim
Climate - Hot and Dry
Int. Dialling Code - Int. + 966

SEYCHELLES
Capital - Victoria
Language - Creole, French, English
Currency - Seychelles Rupee
Religion - Roman Catholic
Climate - Tropical
Int. Dialling Code - Int. + 248
UK Tourist Office - 020 7224 1670

SINGAPORE
Capital - Singapore City
Language - Malay, Chinese, English, Tamil (All Official)
Currency - Singapore Dollar
Religion - Buddhist, Christian, Muslim, Hindu, Taoist,- Multi religious
Climate - Equatorial
Int. Dialling Code - Int. + 65

SLOVAK REPUBLIC
Capital - Bratislava
Language - Slovak (Official)
Currency - New Koruna
Religion - Roman Catholic, Lutheran
Climate - Continental, hot summers and cold winters
Int. Dialling Code - Int. + 42

SLOVENIA
Capital - Ljubljana
Language - Slovene
Currency - Tolar
Religion - Roman Catholic
Climate - Continental
Int. Dialling Code - Int. + 386
UK Tourist Office - 020 7372 3767

SOUTH AFRICA
Capital - Pretoria
Language - Afrikaans, English (Both Official)
Currency - Rand
Religion - Christian, Muslim, Hindu, and tribal religions
Climate - Temperate
Int. Dialling Code - Int. + 27
UK Tourist Office - 020 8944 8080

SPAIN
Capital - Madrid
Language - Spanish
Currency - Peseta

Religion - Roman Catholic
Climate - Mediterranean in the south also the east coast, temperate elsewhere
Int. Dialling Code - Int. + 34
UK Tourist Office - 020 7499 0901

SRI LANKA
Capital - Colombo
Language - Sinhala, Tamil, English
Currency - Sri Lankan Rupee
Religion - Buddhist, Hindu, Muslim, Christian
Climate - Tropical
Int. Dialling Code - Int. + 94
UK Tourist Office - 020 7262 1841

SWEDEN
Capital - Stockholm
Language - Swedish
Currency - Krona
Religion - Lutheran
Climate - Hot summers, cold winters
Int. Dialling Code - Int. + 46
UK Tourist Office - 020 7724 5869

SWITZERLAND
Capital - Bern
Language - German, French, Italian
Currency - Swiss Franc
Religion - Roman Catholic, Protestant
Climate - Warm summers, Cold winters
Int. Dialling Code - Int. + 41
UK Tourist Office - 020 7734 4577

SYRIA
Capital - Damascus
Language - Arabic
Currency - Syrian Pound
Religion - Muslim
Climate - Very Hot and Dry inland, Mediterranean on the coast
Int. Dialling Code - Int. + 963

TAIWAN
Capital - Taipei
Language - Mandarin Chinese (Official), other Chinese dialects
Currency - New Taiwan Dollar
Religion - Confucianist, Buddhist
Climate - Subtropical
Int. Dialling Code - Int. + 886

TANZANIA
Capital - Dar es Salam
Language - Kiswahili, English
Currency - Tanzanian Shilling
Religion - Tribal, Muslim, Christian
Climate - Tropical
Int. Dialling Code - Int. + 255
UK Tourist Office - 020 7407 0566

THAILAND
Capital - Bangkok
Language - Thai, Chinese (Both Official)
Currency - Baht
Religion - Buddhist
Climate - Tropical, monsoon season from May to October
Int. Dialling Code - Int. + 66
UK Tourist Office - 020 7499 7679

TRINIDAD AND TOBAGO
Capital - Port of Spain
Language - English (Official)
Currency - Trinidad and Tobago Dollar
Religion - Roman Catholic, Hindu, Protestant
Climate - Tropical
Int. Dialling Code - Int. + 1809
UK Tourist Office - 020 8367 3752

TUNISIA
Capital - Tunis
Language - Arabic (Official), French
Currency - Dinar
Religion - Muslim
Climate - Hot and Dry inland, Temperate on the coast
Int. Dialling Code - Int. + 216
UK Tourist Office - 020 7224 5598

TURKEY
Capital - Ankara
Language - Turkish (Official), Arabic, Kurdish
Currency - Turkish Lira
Religion - Muslim
Climate - Mediterranean
Int. Dialling Code - Int. + 90
UK Tourist Office - 020 7629 7771

UGANDA
Capital - Kampala
Language - English (Official), Luganda, Lwo, Swahili, Ateso
Currency - Uganda New Shilling
Religion - Roman Catholic, Protestant, Muslim
Climate - Tropical, cooler on the higher ground
Int. Dialling Code - Int. + 256

UKRAINE
Capital - Kiev
Language - Ukrainian
Currency - Grivna
Religion - Ukrainian Orthodox
Climate - Temperate
Int. Dialling Code - Int. + 380

UNITED ARAB EMIRATES
Capital - Abu Dhabi
Language - Arabic (Official)
Currency - United Arab Emirates Dirham
Religion - Muslim
Climate - Hot, cool in the winter
Int. Dialling Code - Int. + 971
UK Tourist Office - 020 7839 0580

UNITED KINGDOM
Capital - London
Language - English
Currency - Pound Sterling
Religion - Christian
Climate - Temperate
Int. Dialling Code - Int. + 44
UK Tourist Office - 020 8846 9000

UNITED STATES OF AMERICA
Capital - Washington DC
Language - English, Spanish
Currency - US Dollar
Religion - Christian
Climate - Subtropical in the south, Hot summers and Cold winters in the north
Int. Dialling Code - Int. + 1
UK Tourist Office - 01891 600530

URUGUAY
Capital - Montevideo
Language - Spanish
Currency - Nuevo Peso
Religion - Roman Catholic
Climate - Temperate
Int. Dialling Code - Int. + 598

VATICAN CITY STATE
Capital - Vatican City
Language - Latin (Official), Italian
Currency - Vatican City Lira, Italian Lira
Religion - Roman Catholic
Climate - Mediterranean
Int. Dialling Code - Int. + 39

VENEZUELA
Capital - Caracas
Language - Spanish (Official)
Currency - Bolivar
Religion - Roman Catholic
Climate - Tropical
Int. Dialling Code - Int. + 58

VIETNAM
Capital - Hanoi
Language - Vietnamese (Official)
Currency - Rial
Religion - Buddhist
Climate - Tropical
Int. Dialling Code - Int. + 84

YEMEN
Capital - Sanaa
Language - Arabic
Currency - Rial
Religion - Muslim
Climate - Hot and Humid
Int. Dialling Code - Int. + 967

ZAMBIA
Capital - Lusaka
Language - English (Official), local languages
Currency - Kwacha
Religion - Christian
Climate - Tropical
Int. Dialling Code - Int. + 260
UK Tourist Office - 020 7589 6343

ZIMBABWE
Capital - Harare
Language - English (Official), Shona, Sindebele
Currency - Zimbabwe Dollar
Religion - Christian, Muslim, Hindu
Climate - Subtropical
Int. Dialling Code - Int + 263
UK Tourist Office - 020 7240 6169

CLIMATE DEFINITIONS

Tropical - High temperatures and heavy rainfall throughout the year.

Subtropical - High temperatures throughout the year in association with extremely varied rainfall, particularly associated with monsoon regions of the world.

Hot - Temperatures that exceed 100 degrees and where rainfall is less than 10 inches / 250 mm per year.

Mediterranean - Hot and dry summers, mild moist winters.

Temperate - Rainfall and temperature are evenly distributed throughout the year, but the day to day weather of a country with a temperate climate is extremely changeable.

Equatorial - Always warm and moist.

Monsoon - Rain at one part of the year and a dry season at the other part of the year. Temperatures range more widely, especially in the dry season.

Continental - The summers are hot and the winters are very cold. The summers bring rain and thunderstorms, and the winters bring frost and varying amounts of snow.

Arctic - Variable climate. The summer months (May to July) brings quiet, overcast and sometimes foggy weather. The temperatures at the height of the summer (July) can get to freezing or just above freezing. The autumn is the most variable season with snow and gales.

Weights and Measures

In this small section, you will find a list of conversion tables for calculating weights and measures, that people associated with the travel and tourism industry may encounter.

KEY:

oz = ounce / ounces
g = gram / gramme / grammes
Kg = Kilogram / Kilogramme
Kgs = Kilogrammes
lb = pound
lbs = pounds
Km = Kilometre(s)
in = inch
mm = millimetre / millimeter
ft = foot / feet
m = metre / meter

WEIGHT

1 oz= 28.35g
1g= 0.04oz

1lb= 0.45Kgs
1Kg= 2.20lbs

1 Ton = 1.02 Tonnes
1 Tonne = 0.98 Tons

DISTANCE

1 Mile = 1.61 km
1 km = 0.62 Miles

LENGTH

1 in = 25 mm
1 ft = 305 mm
10 ft = 3.05 m
10 mm = 0.394 in
1m = 3.281 ft

AREA

1 Acre = 0.405 Hectares
1 Hectare = 2.471 Acres

CAPACITY

1 USA fluid oz = 0.030 metric litre
1 imperial fluid oz = 0.028 metric litre
8 USA fluid oz = 1/2 Pint
10 imperial fluid oz = 1/2 Pint
16 USA fluid oz = 1 Pint
20 Imperial fluid oz = 1 Pint
2 Pints = 1 Quart
1 Quart = 0.946 metric litre
1 Quart = 1.137 metric litres
4 Quart = 1 USA Gallon
4 Quart = 1 Imperial Gallon
1 USA Gallon = 3.785 metric litres
1 Imperial Gallon = 4.546 metric litres

AIRLINE CODINGS

The major airlines of the world

Key: * = National Carrier

A

AA American Airlines (US)
AC Air Canada *
AF Air France*
AH Air Algerie*
AI Air India*
AIH Air Tours
AM Aeromexico*
AN Ansett Australian Airlines
AO Aviaco (Spain)
AR Aerolineas Argentinas*
AT Royal Air Maroc (Morocco)*
AV Avianca (Colombia)*
AY Finnair (Finland)*
AZ Alitalia (Italy)*

B

BA British Airways
BB Balair (Switzerland)
BD British Midland
BG Biman Bangladesh Airlines*
BI Royal Brunei Airlines*
BP Air Botswana*
BR EVA Airlines (Taiwan)
BU Braathens (Norway)
BW BWIA - British West Indian Airlines (Trinidad and Tobago)*
BY Britannia Airlines (UK)
BZ Buzz

C

CA Air China
CI China Airlines
CK Gambia Airlines*
CO Continental Airlines (USA)
CP Canadian Airlines
CU Cubana (Cuba)*
CX Cathay Pacific (Hong Kong)
CY Cyprus Airways*

D

DL Delta Airlines (USA)
DM Maersk Air (Denmark)
DP Air 2000 (UK)
DS Air Senegal*
DY Alyemda - Yemen Airlines (South Yemen)*
D6 Inter Air (UK)

E

EI Air Lingus*
EK Emirates (United Arab Emirates)*
EL Air Nippon (Japan)
ET Ethiopian Airlines*
EZY Easy Jet

F

FF Tower Air (USA)
FI Icelandair*
FR Ryanair (Ireland)
FV Viva Air (Spain)

G

GA Garuda Indonesia*
GF Gulf Air (Bahrain)
GH Ghana Airways*
GOE Go
GU Aviateca (Guatemala)*

H

HA Haiwaian Airlines*
HM Air Seychelles*
HP America West Airlines (USA)
HV Transavia Airlines (The Netherlands)

I

IB Iberia (Spain)*

IC Indian Airlines
IR Iran Air*
IT Air Inter (France)
IY Yemenia - Yemen Airlines (North Yemen)*

J
JD Japan Air System
JE Manx Air (UK)
JK Spanair (Spain)
JL JAL-Japan Airlines*
JP Adria Airlines (Slovenia)
JY Jersey European

K
KA Dragonair (Hong Kong)
KE Korean Air (South Korea)
KJ British Mediterranean Airways
KL KLM - Royal Dutch Airlines (The Netherlands)
KM Air Malta
KQ Kenya Airways*
KU Kuwait Airways*
KX Cayman Airways*

L
LA LAN - Chile*
LG Luxair (Luxembourg)*
LH Lufthansa (Germany)*
LO LOT - Polish Airlines*
LT L.T.U. International Airlines (Germany)
LX Crossair (Switzerland)
LY El Al Israel Airlines*
LZ Balkan (Bulgaria)*
L6 Air Maldives*

M
MA MALEV Hungarian Airlines*
ME MEA - Middle East Airlines (Lebanon)*
MH Malaysia Airlines*
MJ LAPA (Paraguay)*
MK Air Muritius*
MP Martinair (The Netherlands)
MS Egyptair*
MX Mexicana Airlines (Mexico)

N
NG Lauda Air (Austria)
NH All Nippon Airways (Japan)
NW North West Airlines (USA)
NZ Air New Zealand*

O
OA Olympic Airways (Greece)*
OK CSA - Czechoslovak Airlines*
OM MIAT - Mongolian Airlines*
OS Austrian Airlines*
OU Croatia Airlines*
OV Estonia Air*

P
PK Pakistan International Airlines*
PL Aeropreu*
PR Philippine Airlines*

Q
QF Qantas Airways (Australia)*
QU Uganda Airlines*

R
RA Royal Nepal Airlines*
RB Syrian Arab Airlines*
RG VARIG (Brazil)*
RJ Royal Jordanian Airlines*
RK Air Afrique
RO TAROM (Romania)*

S
SA South African Airways*
SD Sudan Airways*
SK SAS - Scandanavian Airlines System*
SN Sabena Belgian World Airlines*
SQ Singapore Airlines*
SR Swisssair (Switzerland)*
SU Aeroflot (Russia)*
SV Saudia (Saudia Arabia)*
SW Air Namibia*

T

TA Taca International Airlines (El Salvador)*
TG Thai Airways International*
TK Turkish Airlines*
TP TAP Air Portugal*
TQ Transwede Airways (Sweden)
TU Tunis Air (Tunisia)*
TW TWA (USA)
TZ America Trans Air (USA)

U

UA United Airlines (USA)
UK KLM (UK)
UM Air Zimbabwe*
US US Air (USA)
UX Air Europa

V

VA VIASA (Venezuela)*
VD Air Liberte (France)
VK Virgin Express
VN Vietnam Airlines*
VS Virgin Atlantic (UK)

W

WG Taiwan Airlines
WH China North West Airlines
WN Southwest Airlines (USA)
WO World Airways (USA)
WT Nigeria Airways*

X

X2 China Xinhua Airlines

Y

YK Cyprus Turkish Airlines
YP Aero Lloyd (Germany)

Z

ZB Monarch Airlines (UK)
ZQ Ansett New Zealand
Z9 Aero Zambia*

AIRPORT / CITY CODINGS

The major airports and cities throughout the world.

A

AAH-Aarhus-Denmark
ABQ-Albuquerque-USA
ABS-Abu Simbel-Egypt
ABZ-Aberdeen-United Kingdom
ACE-Lanzarote-Canary Islands
ADB-Izmir-Turkey
ADD-Addis Ababa-Ethiopia
ADE-Aden-South Yemen
ADL-Adelaide-Australia
AEP-Jorge Newbery-Argentina
AGA-Agadir-Morocco
AGP-Malaga-Spain
AIY-Atlantic City-USA
AKL-Auckland-New Zealand
ALB-Albany, New York-USA
ALC-Alicante-Spain
ALG-Algiers-Algeria
AMM-Amman-Jordan
AMS-Amsterdam-The Netherlands
ANC-Anchorage, Alaska-USA
ANK-Ankara-Turkey
ANR-Antwerp-Belgium
ANU-Antigua-Leeward Islands, West Indies
AQJ-Aqaba-Jordan
ARN-Stockholm-Sweden
ASE -Aspen, Colorado-USA
ASU-Asuncion-Paraguay
ATH-Athens-Greece
ATL-Atlanta, Georgia-USA
AUH-Abu Dhabi-United Arab Emirates
AYQ-Ayers Rock-Australia

B

BAH-Bahrain-Bahrain
BAJ-Bali-Papua New Guinea
BBU-Bucharest-Romania
BCN-Barcelona-Spain
BDA-Bermuda-Bermuda

BEY-Beirut-Lebanon
BFS-Belfast-United Kingdom
BGI-Barbados-Barbados, West Indies
BGO-Bergen-Norway
BHX-Birmingham-United Kingdom
BHZ-Belo Horizonte-Brazil
BIO-Bilbao-Spain
BJL-Banjul-Gambia
BJS-Beijing-China
BKK-Bangkok-Thailand
BLL-Billund-Denmark
BLQ-Bologna-Italy
BLR-Bangalore-India
BMA-Stockholm, Bromma-Sweden
BNE-Brisbane-Australia
BNJ-Bonn-Germany
BOD-Bordeaux-France
BOG-Bogota-Colombia
BOM-Mumbai-India
BOS-Boston, MA-USA
BRE- Bremen-Germany
BRI-Bari-Italy
BRN-Berne-Switzerland
BRQ-Brno-Czech Republic
BRS-Bristol-United Kingdom
BRU-Brussels-Belgium
BSB-Brasilia-Brazil
BSL-Basle-Switzerland
BTS-Bratislava-Slovak Republic
BUD-Budapest-Hungary
BUE-Buenos Aires-Argentina
BUH-Bucharest-Romania
BWI-Baltimore, MD-USA
BWN-Bandar Seri Begawan-Brunei

C

CAG-Cagliari-Italy (Sicily)
CAI-Cairo-Egypt
CAS-Casablanca-Morocco
CBR-Camberra-Australia
CCU-Calcutta-India
CGH-Sao Paulo-Brazil
CGK-Jakarta-Indonesia
CGN-Cologne-Germany
CIA-Rome (Ciampino)-Italy
CLE-Cleveland, OH-USA
CLT-Charlotte, NC-USA
CMB-Colombo-Sri Lanka
CMN-Casablanca-Morocco
CNF-Belo Horizonte-Brazil
CNS-Cairns-Australia
COR-Cordoba-Argentina
CPH-Copenhagen-Denmark
CPT-Cape Town-South Africa
CUN-Cancun-Mexico
CVG-Cincinnati, OH-USA
CWL-Cardiff-UK
CXH-Vancouver-Canada

D

DAC-Dhaka-Bangladesh
DAM-Damascus-Syria
DAR-Dar-es-Salaam-Tanzania
DEL-Delhi-India
DEN-Denver, CO-USA
DFW-Dallas F/W, TX-USA
DHA-Dhahran-Saudi Arabia
DLM-Dalaman -Turkey
DOH-Dohar-Qatar
DRS-Dresden-Germany
DRW-Darwin-Australia
DTM-Dortmund-Germany
DTT-Detroit, MI-USA
DUB-Dublin-Ireland
DUR-Durban-South Africa
DUS-Dusseldorf-Germany
DXB-Dubai-United Arab Emirates

E

EAB-San Sebastian-Spain
EBB-Entebbe (Kampala)-Uganda
EDI-Edinburgh-United Kingdom
EIN-Eindhoven-The Netherlands
ELP-El Paso, TX-USA
EMA-East Midlands-United Kingdom
EWR-New York/ Newark-USA
EYW-Key West, FL-USA
EZE-Ministro Pistarini, Buenos Aries-Argentina

F

FAO-Faro-Portugal
FCO-Rome Leonardo da Vinci-Italy
FIH-Kinshasa-Zaire
FLL-Fort Lauderdale, FL-USA
FLR-Florence-Italy
FMO-Munster-Germany
FNA-Freetown-Sierra Leone
FNC-Funchal-Medeira
FNJ-Pyongyang-North Korea
FPO-Freeport-Bahamas
FRA-Frankfurt-Germany

G

GCI-Guernsey-United Kingdom
GM-Grand Cayman-Cayman Islands
GDL-Guadalajara-Mexico
GDN-Gdansk-Poland
GEO- Georgetown-Guyana
GIB-Gibraltar-Gibraltar
GIG-Rio de Janeiro-Brazil
GLA-Glasgow-United Kingdom
GNB-Grenoble-France
GOA-Genoa-Italy
GOT-Gothenburg-Sweden
GRU-Sao Paulo-Brazil
GRX-Granada-Spain
GRZ-Graz-Austria
GUA-Guatemala City-Guatemala
GVA-Geneva-Switzerland
GWY-Galway-Ireland
GYE-Guayaquil-Ecuador

H

HAJ-Hanover-Germany
HAM-Hamburg-Germany
HAN-Hanoi-Vietnam
HAV-Havana-Cuba
HBA-Hobart (Tasmania)-Australia
HDD-Hyderabad-Pakistan
HEL-Helsinki-Finland
HER-Heraklion (Crete)-Greece
HFA-Haifa-Israel
HIJ-Hiroshima-Japan
HKG-Hong Kong (Kai Tak)-Hong Kong
HKT-Phuket-Thailand
HND-Tokyo (Haneda)-Japan
HNL-Honolulu, HI-USA
HOU-Houston, TX-USA
HRE-Harare-Zimbabwe
HUY-Humberside-United Kingdom

I

IAD-Washington (Dulles)-USA
IBZ-Ibiza-Spain
IEV-Kiev-Ukraine
IND-Indianapolis, IN-USA
INN-Innsbruck-Austria
INV-Inverness-United Kingdom
IOM-Isle of Man-United Kingdom
ISB-Islamabad-Pakistan
IST-Istanbul-Turkey
ITM-Osaka (Itami)-Japan
IZM-Izmir-Turkey

J

JAX -Jacksonville, FL-USA
JED-Jeddah-Saudi Arabia
JER-Jersey-United Kingdom
JFK-New York (JFK)-USA
JIB-Djibouti-Djibouti
JKT-Jakarta-Indonesia
JNB-Johannesburg-South Africa
JRS-Jerusalem
JSI-Skiathos-Greece

K

KGL-Kigali-Rwanda
KGS-Kos-Greece
KHI-Karachi-Pakistan
KIN-Kingston-Jamaica
KIX-Osaka (Kansai)-Japan
KRK-Krakow-Poland
KTM-Katmandu-Nepal
KUL-Kuala Lumpar-Malaysia
KWI-Kuwait-Kuwait

L

LAD-Luanda-Angola
LAS-Las Vegas-USA

LAX-Los Angeles-USA
LBA-Leeds/Bradford-United Kingdom
LBV-Libreville-Gabon
LCA-Larnaca-Cyprus
LCY-London City-United Kingdom
LDY-Londonderry-United Kingdom
LED-St. Petersburg-Russia
LEH-Le Havre-France
LEI-Almeira-Spain
LEJ-Leipzig-Germany
LFW-Lome-Togo
LGA-New York (La Guardia) USA
LGB-Long Beach, CA-USA
LGG-Liege-Belgium
LGW-London Gatwick-United Kingdom
LHE-Lahore-Pakistan
LHR-London Heathrow-United Kingdom
LIL-Lille-France
LIM-Lima-Peru
LIN-Milan (Linate)-Italy
LIS-Lisbon-Portugal
LJU-Ljubljana-Slovenia
LNZ-Linz-Austria
LOS-Lagos-Nigeria
LPA-Gran Canaria-Canary Islands
LPB-La Paz-Bolivia
LPL-Liverpool-United Kingdom
LTN-London Luton-United Kingdom
LUG-Lugano-Switzerland
LUN-Lusaka-Zambia
LUX-Luxembourg-Luxembourg
LXR-Luxor-Egypt
LYP-Faisalabad-Pakistan
LYS-Lyon-France

M

MAA Madras-India
MAD-Madrid-Spain
MAH-Menorca-Spain
MAN-Manchester-United Kingdom
MBA-Mombasa-Kenya
MBJ-Montego Bay-Jamaica
MCI-Kansas City-USA
MCO-Orlando-USA
MCT-Muscat-Oman
MDE-Medellin-Colombia
MEL-Melbourne-Australia
MEM-Memphis-USA
MEX-Mexico City-Mexico
MGQ-Mogadishu-Somalia
MIA-Miami-USA
MIR-Monastir-Tunisia
MJV-Murcia-Spain
MKE-Milwaukee-USA
MLH-Mulhouse-France
MLW-Monrovia-Liberia
MME-Teeside-United Kingdom
MMX-Malmo-Sweden
MNI-Montserrat-Montserrat
MNL-Manila-Philippines
MPL-Montpellier-France
MRS-Marseille-France
MRU-Mauritius-Mauritius
MSP-Minneapolis, MN-USA
MSQ-Minsk-Belarus
MST-Maastricht-The Netherlands
MSY-New Orleans, LA-USA
MTY-Monterrey-Mexico
MUC-Munich-Germany
MVD-Montevideo-Uruguay
MXP-Milan (Malpensa)-Italy

N

NAP-Naples-Italy
NAS-Nassau-Bahamas
NBO-Nairobi-Kenya
NCE-Nice-France
NCL-Newcastle-United Kingdom
NGO-Nagoya-Japan
NGS-Nagasaki-Japan
NRT-Tokyo (Narita)-Japan
NTE-Nantes-France
NTY-Sun City-South Africa
NUE-Nuremberg-Germany

O

OAK-Oakland, CA-USA
ODE-Odense-Denmark
OKA-Okinawa-Japan
OKC-Oklahoma City-USA

OKD-Sapporo-Japan
OPO-Porto-Portugal
ORD-Chicago (O'Hare)-USA
ORY-Paris (Orly)-France
OTP-Bucharest (Otopeni)-Romania

P
PAP-Port au Prince-Haiti
PEK-Beijing-China
PEN-Penang-Malaysia
PER-Perth-Australia
PGF-Perpignan-France
PHL-Philadelphia, PA-USA
PHX-Phoenix, AZ-USA
PIK-Glasgow (Prestwick)-United Kingdom
PIT-Pittsburgh, PA-USA
PMF-Parma-Italy
PMI-Palma de Mallorca-Spain
PMO-Palermo-Italy
PNM-Phnom-Penh-Cambodia
POM-Port Moresby-Papua New Guinea
POS-Port of Spain-Trinidad and Tobago
PSA-Pisa-Italy
PTY-Panama City (Tocumen)-Panama

R
RBA-Rabat -Morocco
REC-Recife-Brazil
RHO-Rhodes-Greece
RIX-Riga-Latvia
RKV-Reykjavik-Iceland
RMI-Rimini-Italy
RTM-Rotterdam-The Netherlands
RUH-Riyadh-Saudi Arabia

S
SAH-Sana'a-North Yemen
SAL-San Salvador-El Salvador
SAN-San Diego, CA-USA
SAT-San Antonio,-TX-USA
SCL-Santiago-Chile
SDQ-Santa Domingo-Dominican Republic
SDR-Santander-Spain
SDU-Rio deJaneiro-Brazil
SDV-Tel Aviv-Israel
SEA-Seattle, WA-USA
SEL-Soeul (Kimpo)-South Korea
SFO-San Francisco, CA-USA
SGN-Ho Chi Minh City-Vietnam
SIN-Singpore-Singapore
SJO-San Jose-Costa Rica
SJU-San Juan-Puerto Rico
SKG-Thessaloniki-Greece
SOF-Sofia-Bulgaria
SSA-Salvador-Brazil
STN-London (Stansted)-United Kingdom
STR-Stuttgart-Germany
SVG-Stavanger-Norway
SVO- Moscow (Sheremetyevo)-Russia
SVQ-Seville-Spain
SXB-Strasbourg-France
SXF-Berlin (Schonefeld)-Germany
SYD-Sydney-Australia
SZG-Salzburg-Austria

T
TFN-Tenerife- Norte) -Canary Islands
TFS-Tenerife- (Reina Sofia) - Canary Islands
TGU-Tegucigalpa-Honduras
THF-Berlin (Tempelhof)-Germany
THR-Tehran-Iran
TIA-Tirana-Albania
TKS-Tokushima-Japan
TLL-Tallin-Estonia
TLS -Toulouse-France
TLV-Tel Aviv (Ben Gurion)-Israel
TNG-Tangier-Morocco
TNR-Antananarivo-Madagascar
TPA-Tampa, FL-USA
TPE-Taipei (Kai Chek)-Taiwan
TRN-Turin-Italy
TUL-Tulsa, OK-USA
TUN-Tunis-Tunisia
TUS-Tuscon, AZ-USA
TXL-Berlin (Tegel)-Germany

U
UIO-Quito-Ecuador

ULN-Ulan Bator-Mongolia
UME-Umea-Sweden

V
VCE-Venice-Italy
VLC-Valencia-Spain
VNO-Vilnius-Lithuania
VRN-Verona-Italy

W
WAW-Warsaw-Poland
WDH-Windhoek-Namibia
WLG-Wellington-New Zealand

X
XRY-Jerez-Spain

Y
YEG-Edmonton-Canada
YHZ-Halifax-Canada
YMX-Montreal (Mirabel)-Canada
YOW-Ottawa-Canada
YUL-Montreal (Dorval)-Canada
YVR-Vancouver-Canada
YYC-Calgary-Canada
YYJ-Victoria-Canada
YYZ-Toronto-Canada

Z
ZAG-Zagreb-Croatia
ZAZ-Zaragoza-Spain
ZRH-Zurich-Switzerland